D1124799

John Mackinlay

Globalisation and Insurgency

Adelphi Paper 352

Oxford University Press, Great Clarendon Street, Oxford OX2 6DP
Oxford   New York
Athens   Auckland   Bangkok   Bombay   Calcutta   Cape Town
Dar es Salaam   Delhi   Florence   Hong Kong   Istanbul   Karachi
Kuala Lumpur   Madras   Madrid   Melbourne   Mexico City
Nairobi   Paris   Taipei   Tokyo   Toronto
and associated companies in
Ibadan

Oxford is a trade mark of Oxford University Press

Published in the United States
by Oxford University Press Inc., New York

© The International Institute for Strategic Studies 2002

First published November 2002 by **Oxford University Press** for
The International Institute for Strategic Studies
Arundel House, 13–15 Arundel Street, Temple Place, London WC2R 3DX
www.iiss.org

Director John Chipman
Editor Mats R. Berdal
Assistant Editor Matthew Foley

British Library Cataloguing in Publication Data
Data available

Library of Congress Cataloguing in Publication Data

ISBN 0-19-852707-1
ISSN 0567-932x

Contents

Tables and Charts

Glossary

ADFL	Alliance of Democratic Forces for the Liberation of the Congo
AFL	Armed Forces of Liberia
AFRC	Armed Forces Revolutionary Council
CEO	chief executive officer
CMF	Commonwealth Monitoring Force
ETA	Euskada ta Askatasuna (Basque separatists)
GPS	global positioning system
IRA	Irish Republican Army
IT	information technology
ITU	International Telecommunications Union
LTTE	Liberation Tigers of Tamil Eelam
MAK	Maktab al-Khidmat
NATO	North Atlantic Treaty Organisation
NCO	non-commissioned officer
NGO	non-governmental organisation
NPFL	National Patriotic Front of Liberia
PLO	Palestine Liberation Organisation
RUF	Revolutionary United Front
RUFP	Revolutionary United Front Party
SAS	Special Air Service
SPLA	Sudan People's Liberation Army
UNITA	National Union for the Total Independence of Angola

Introduction

During the Cold War, each side studied its enemies carefully. The real versions of these enemies stood on opposing sides of the inner-German border, replete with armoured columns and missiles. But far behind the Central European lines, there were replicas or models created for training purposes. In the case of NATO, Warsaw Pact forces were labelled 'Fantasians', and the Chinese 'Vandals'. These were used as a basis for planning NATO exercises; manuals explained their organisation, weapon systems and tactics.[1] Beyond NATO's flank, a different enemy, the insurgent, was also being studied and conceptualised, but without pseudonyms and with greater directness. From 1965 to 1995, a series of British military manuals described the insurgents' general characteristics, how they operated and how government forces should deal with them.[2]

As the new strategic era began to unfold in the 1990s, UN forces, comprising units from NATO and the former Warsaw Pact, found themselves intervening in Cambodia, the Balkans and Somalia. They came ostensibly as peace guarantors, or as protectors of humanitarian relief. In these complex interventions, international forces were mandated and configured to act in a peacekeeping role, on a neutral basis, interposing themselves between the parties in a conflict, but not taking action against a particular faction. In appearance, nomenclature and intent, these international forces were derived from traditional peacekeeping of a previous era. However, in practical terms the situation had changed and become more complicated; interventions now involved an array of different actors and international organisations. These saw themselves as observers, referees, even-handed distributors of humanitarian relief, human-rights investigators, fund-raisers and dispensers and development consultants, but not as the opponents of the local forces which regularly obstructed them.

When the UN's post-Cold War interventions had failed or partially failed due to such confrontation, military contributors began to understand that their role required a less supine, more adversarial approach. The purpose was no longer simply to behave in the manner of a harmless referee between supposedly consenting factions, but to act, partially if necessary, to restore the monopoly of violence. Although the UN's international forces continued to deploy with the nomenclature, appearance and body language of peacekeepers, regional forces, sometimes acting without the full backing of the UN Security Council, began to adopt a more muscular approach. This trend away from the peacekeeping ethic was manifested in practical terms in the operations of sub-regional forces, which attempted to stabilise civil violence and assist humanitarian efforts in the Balkans, West Africa and the 'former Soviet space'. In military terms, these forces had a more aggressive posture and a ready-for-combat appearance on the ground. Not all were completely successful, but in a rough-and-ready manner most managed to restore order locally. At the same time, Western European doctrine began to change. Led by the British and then the Nordic countries, new doctrines were published which in turn encouraged sub-regional security organisations to move towards a more convincing military deployment.[3] Some defence forces were now altering their instructions for training and operations to reflect the possibility of contested operations. Whereas traditional peacekeepers remained careful not to identify an 'enemy', the presence of weapon systems associated with more effective military operations implied the presence of 'hostile forces'.

In military logic, the critical path of doctrine development begins with an attempt to conceptualise the threat or risk, which at the soldier's level will be simplified to a description of the opponent's characteristics. Understanding the 'enemy' and his tactics is the first essential for training and operational planning. But in the newly-emerging doctrines of the 1990s, this information was missing.[4] There has been no attempt to conceptualise an adversary. In the post-Cold War period, when civilian casualties were so much higher due to displacement, genocide and conflict-related deprivation, the need to counter insurgent forces became a much greater priority for major armies. Yet their conceptual clarity and insight on insurgency was (and still is) less developed. During the 1990s, it was academics and the media who attempted to define insurgency, not the international contingents which were already engaged to contain it. This analytical gap was additionally complicated by global change and the ramifications of a new strategic era.

This paper provides a step towards achieving a more universal understanding of insurgent forces in the post-Cold War period, which could act as a guide for future international forces. The first chapter shows how the effects of globalisation have gradually changed the relationship between weak governments and the insurgent forces that seek to oppose them, debilitating governments and enriching insurgent leaders. It has become increasingly possible for insurgent forces with untrained military units to succeed in challenging a dysfunctional government. In the second chapter, the conditions which dictate the idiosyncratic nature of each insurgent force are analysed more closely: the terrain, the population and, above all, the amount of wealth which can be mobilised to sustain prolonged violence. The central proposition of this paper is that globalisation has stretched the definitions of insurgency, and created several different types of insurgent force. In the third chapter these are categorised, not so much by their political intent as by their organisation and military potency. Four broad categories emerge. Lumpen insurgents are loosely organised armed bands which may succeed against a weakened government. Clan forces are defined by their long-standing family or clan structures, which can be mobilised for conflict into primitive military units that are suitable for raiding, but not sustained fighting. Popular insurgencies are distinguished by their more developed ideologies and a much closer relationship with the elements of the population that support their ideology. They also tend to be militarily more organised and therefore more dangerous to those who oppose them from beyond the immediate crisis zone. The bin Laden phenomenon has created a fourth category, the global insurgency. In this case, the military organisation spans several regions and draws support from a huge diaspora that shares an ideology or a religion. Global insurgents have a long reach and are assisted by the misdirected energy of the international media, which amplify and communicate the impact of their actions to their supporters. The obvious corollary to the expanding definitions of insurgency is that each category requires a different counter-strategy. In the 1990s, the absence of definitions encouraged a 'one-fix' approach that overestimates the competence of the Lumpen insurgent, and underestimates the international dimension of the global insurgent. The conclusion suggests that each category of insurgent requires a specific counter-strategy. Some general principles emerge from current operations that are relevant to all categories; furthermore, if these are applied with greater determination, they may begin to alter the character of complex interventions.

This paper adopts the British Army's 1995 definition of insurgency as the 'actions of a minority group within a state who are intent on forcing political change by means of a mixture of subversion, propaganda and military pressure, aiming to persuade or intimidate the broad mass of people to accept such a change'.[5] Although similar to more recent definitions, its significance lies in the recognition of a systemic approach by the insurgent, which requires a similarly systemic counter-strategy. In some failing states, this definition is confused by elements of the government which themselves act in the manner of insurgents, pillaging state resources and terrorising particular communities within the population. But insurgencies should not be seen as uniformly negative. A popular insurgency can be the midwife of a better and more caring regime and, in the case of an uprising against illegal occupation, insurgent forces may be widely supported by the international community. This paper does not set out to identify good and bad insurgencies, but does suggest that they need to be better understood by forces, particularly international forces, which seek to contain them in order to promote a peace process. In the media, the word 'terrorism' is sometimes used synonymously with insurgency. However, in this paper the UK doctrinal distinction between insurgency and terrorism is upheld. 'Terrorism' therefore refers to the 'use of indiscriminate violence to intimidate the general majority of people in a state to accept the political changes advocated by the insurgents'. Terrorism is merely the weapon or the tool of the insurgent; it is not a viable concept on its own and cannot be the sole sustaining energy of a long-term campaign or the reason for the support of a population. Terrorism is therefore a tactic within the overall concept of insurgency and, as an abstract concept, it cannot be the objective of a counter-strategy.[6]

Chapter 1

Global Change and Weak States

Government officials and even academics had little opportunity to react analytically to the events of the 1990s. There was no space to stand back and consider how the international tenets of collective action were changing. At the same time, there was also a sense of continuity with the Cold War period. The conflicts which had attracted so much attention during the 1990s had occurred in similarly unstable areas in previous decades. In some respects they resembled the Cold War insurgencies, and it could be argued that the violence was not as dramatically 'new' as some claimed.[1]

Nevertheless, in the perspective of five decades there had been important changes, which influenced the behaviour of actors at the state level. This chapter shows how several separate strands of development altered the conditions both for insurgents, and for the government forces that sought to contain them. These changes occurred at different times: some were immediate, and some evolved over a longer period. In the short term, the immediate impact of the end of the Cold War shifted the focus of power in some states by leaving client regimes unsupported and releasing a tide of Cold War materiel on to global markets. In the longer term, the effects of globalisation changed the nature of the conflict area, strengthening some parties and weakening others, expanding the definitions of portable wealth and resources and altering the military equation between government forces and insurgents in favour of the latter. Distant developments at the strategic level reached down to local communities in the conflict zone, and changed the context of the struggle for power and wealth.

Technical improvements had begun to compress the world long before the 1850s. What are now referred to as global changes were already visible in the 1970s, but by the 1990s they were becoming increasingly significant.[2] Globalisation is a collective term that describes many individual strands of development. According to David Held and Anthony McGrew, it is a process which projects social, political and economic activities across frontiers, and from one region to another.[3] It speeds the transmission of ideas, goods, information and capital and the migration of populations, so that distant events alter the lives of isolated communities, whose dependence on foreign investment and influences has increased.

This paper examines how global change influenced local actors in places that became the crisis zones of the 1990s. Although such zones could be found in every region, the states at the epicentre of the violence tended to be poor, undemocratically governed and in many aspects failing. In particular, four individual strands of development had for some time been altering local communities: improvements in transport technology; the proliferation of information and communications; the deregulation of the international economy and markets; and increased migration. The pace of change was gradual, but over several decades the pressures became enormous. The end of the Cold War was a trigger mechanism, which in weaker states released passions and violence that had been building up for some time. Global developments that were perhaps individually benign coalesced to alter the structures of governance, the possession of wealth and the disposition of military power in the 1990s.

In comparison to the gradual pace of globalisation, the events which signalled a change of strategic era occurred swiftly. In the space of a few years, the inner-German border was removed, the massively powerful Soviet forces in Germany withdrew from their barracks and positions and dispersed, and in 1991 the Warsaw Pact was formally dissolved. The impact of these events was visible and immediate. Moreover, this impact was felt in remote communities and villages in regions far from the Central Front of the

Cold War armies. By the late 1980s, diminishing US–Soviet rivalry left client regimes of both sides without support. According to Jean-Christophe Rufin: 'this lack of international support ha[d] not led guerrilla movements to conclude that they should stop fighting: it just made them realise that their war economies ha[d] to change completely. They moved from relying on political assistance from abroad to a new, more business oriented attitude'.[4] Both government forces and insurgents became illegal dealers in precious woods, gemstones, protected antiques, ivory, jade and the production and trafficking of drugs.[5] In doing so, they rapidly discovered and exploited the advantages presented by global change. At the same time, post-Cold War reductions saw a surge of war materiel on to legal and illegal markets. This went beyond increasing the obvious availability of small arms; entire military units were for hire, with Russian garrisons searching for a raison d'être in former Soviet space, and more immediately for a means of subsistence. Logistics aircraft from the disestablished Soviet air force appeared on the air-charter market, and individual mercenaries gravitated towards the new crisis areas of the 1990s.

Transport technology

In the wilderness areas, a potent development was the advance in technology and the proliferation of new transport systems.[6] Among the poorest elements of the population, where subsistence was a day-to-day struggle, the introduction of new transport technology was one of the most important consequences of globalisation.

Generally, the advances which reduced travel times for the rich, safe countries of the world after 1850 did not reach down to developing countries, where road systems had not yet been developed. Later, internal air transport was too expensive to alter the lives of the majority. In these areas, traditional porterage along rivers and footpaths still moved at less than the best average speed for 1840.[7] Furthermore, the transportation of materials in bulk was greatly limited by the need for mules and porters also to carry their own food. This situation prevailed in many developing areas until the 1990s. In Congo, Laurent Kabila's Alliance of Democratic Forces for the Liberation of the Congo (ADFL) moved at the speed of a handcart, following the traditional porter routes through rural areas.[8] In Myanmar during the campaigns of the late 1980s, both government forces and rebel factions used porterage as the main logistic transport in the conflict zone. The ability to override the limitations imposed by terrain and poor technology was a monopoly which lay in the hands of international corporations and the more powerful armed forces. These were the only actors who could afford to use the large helicopters and heavy transport systems that reached into the heart of the wilderness.

By the end of the Cold War, several developments were eroding this monopoly. In the 1980s, overland communications in developing wilderness areas were improved. In particular, engineering companies came to build or improve road systems, leaving behind plant and cross-country vehicles. The introduction of better vehicles, and more importantly better tracks and sealed roads, increased the tempo of movement and interaction; the handcart was overtaken by the jeep. Post-Cold War military reductions also released 1970s- and 1980s-generation logistics aircraft, vessels and vehicles into deregulated civilian use. On land, new and more powerful cross-country vehicles were reaching the world's most isolated areas. They arrived in many forms, as military equipment and as commercial carriers, and in some cases introduced by international development agencies, which needed cheap and easy-to-maintain logistics vehicles. Meanwhile, cheaper and more powerful commercial vehicles were also reaching some remote areas directly from the retail market, in particular the Nissan minibus, the Isuzu 10 MT truck, the Indian Tata series of logistics carriers and European vehicles, such as Mercedes and Fiats.[9]

In the air, Soviet tactical-support helicopters and strategic transport aircraft were ideally suited for remote areas, where more sophisticated carriers were too expensive and too bound by international safety restrictions. Russian-designed tactical helicopters tended to operate without elaborate support facilities, and consequently cost far less. In the long-haul market, chartered strategic aircraft from the Soviet military fleets connected remote airfields in conflict zones directly to the international systems beyond, introducing a two-way traffic that had either never existed before, or had been the monopoly of governments and international corporations. There was also an increase in the number of small, privately-owned aircraft operating in these areas. Popular models were the small ten-seaters, such as the *Cessna* series, which had an increasingly better short take-off capability. These and the smaller *Antonovs* tended to be run by entrepreneurs, who now operated in the remotest areas from very primitive airfields.

At sea, containerisation benefited international trade by dramatically lowering unit costs and speeding up the movement of cargo. It also enabled the small entrepreneur to move large, illegal cargoes around the world with much greater ease than before. In some cases, the transport costs of moving bulk materials against the stream of international export traffic were considerably lower than the real expense of the journey.[10] Containerisation was also anonymous. An illegal cargo cased along with 6,000 other containers and stacked on the deck of a ship was unlikely to be found, and in most cases impossible to open, until its turn came to be unloaded. In this way, illegal merchandise passed more freely than before; a cargo of weapons for the Irish Republican Army (IRA) coming from Canada, for instance, could be credibly manifested as spare parts for laundry machines. Illegal drugs, manifested as cotton, could be hidden behind a heavy barrier of genuine cotton bales. The container was also large and versatile enough to carry stolen cars, armoured vehicles, helicopters and even human beings.[11] Compared to loose cargo, the speed of delivery through the docks on to the ship was so swift that, for the controlling authorities, detection and interception times were reduced to a matter of hours before the container was loaded and the ship sailed. At the destination, despite its size, the container was inconspicuous and easily moved over long distances by truck. Even physically checking several hundred containers on a modestly-sized cargo ship tended to be a fruitless effort. Anticipatory intelligence became more important. In many cases, weak governments whose authority barely extended to the edges of the capital city did not have the information or power to regulate this movement.[12]

The proliferation of a new generation of transport systems and more capable logistics vehicles meant that a small entrepreneur could reach the innermost areas of a developing state, carrying away much larger tonnages and moving awkward bulk materials. As security eroded, international corporations could no longer control the exploitation of natural resources. Although the poorest were still living at a subsistence level, in the same areas small entrepreneurs were now trading where before it would have been impossible for them to operate.[13] In weakened states, this development was altering the definition of portable resources. As long as the transport of bulk materials and passengers remained the monopoly of the government or their international contractors, illicit 'portable resources' referred to the small amounts of precious minerals which could be carried or smuggled out on a person's back. The proliferation of transport systems in the 1990s, operating locally and internationally, widened the definition to include hardwoods, bulk minerals, off-shore fisheries, agricultural produce and even wild game, which smaller entrepreneurs could now seize and remove on to international markets.

Communications

The second strand of technical development which altered the conflict area is described by some as the communications revolution.[14] This refers to the proliferation of cheaper and more powerful electronic systems, as well as the spread of information technology (IT). As with the improvement of transport technology, electronic communications had already reached remote areas in the late 1800s.[15] In the 1990s, the increase in telephone use and the introduction of new electronic communication systems were the catalyst for many aspects of global change. According to the International Telecommunications Union (ITU), main telephone lines increased from over 500 million (m) in 1990 to a projected 1,100m in 2002. From its introduction in 1990, the mobile phone now has 1,000m subscribers; in the space of a decade, 600m internet users have established and exploited a new dimension of communication.[16]

In the remote areas of weakening states, the impact of this meteoric rise in the use and significance of electronic communications was manifold. Once a system had been purchased, distance no longer decided the cost of communicating electronically. Universally, communications became smaller, more portable, mobile and easier to conceal. Users enjoyed vastly-improved access to networks, any of which could be increasingly interactive and carry other audio and visual services. The consequent tidal wave of information in most cases overwhelmed the individual's capacity for absorption and collation. As a result, new filter systems emerged to find and sift through large amounts of data. Regardless of geography and political constraints, new ideas now took much less time to reach an optimum audience. In this way, culture and new technology moved more swiftly from the rich world to the poor, where in the past it could have taken decades. This proliferation of communications acted against governments that were already weakening for other reasons. The freedom of access and the surge of ideas and information could not be controlled, and laws preventing the circulation of subversive material were impossible to enforce. The control of movement and communication, which sometimes went with the exercise of authority, was disintegrating. Government failure and malpractice was increasingly exposed. Rigorously investigated by international non-government researchers, it was now published and made globally visible on the internet. Internationally, new communications monopolies were emerging. Their reach and influence permeated across the world, and their wealth and power considerably exceeded that of many developing states. The internationalisation of these systems was also emphasised by the increasing use of English. By 1999, almost 80% of website and internet stations were in English; one person in six was learning English as a second language.[17] But at the poorest levels in developing countries, the vast majority were excluded from these developments. In some states, the cost of purchasing the basic hardware to join the internet was more than eight years' salary for an average labourer.[18]

IT threatened individual privacy; the compilation of voice features, technical fingerprinting and even credit-card records could be used intrusively against particular suspects. However, these technologies relied on sophisticated and expensive surveillance systems. Thus, despite the intrusive nature of IT, in many states where surveillance was minimal the communications revolution favoured the small entrepreneur, the criminal and the insurgent. The cost of starting a new business was falling dramatically, and small companies with almost no capital now offered services which in the past had been the monopoly of giant firms. For criminal and seditious transactions, the internet opened up a new highway of evasion; it could 'carry illegal material across international borders, covering its electronic tracks, and deliver it straight to the desktops of millions of individuals ... Services could migrate to countries where laws were lenient or weakly enforced, creating offshore havens for pornography, gambling and tax evasion, and breaching international rules on intellectual property'.[19]

Deregulation of the international economy

The third strand of development was the weakening of international commercial systems and markets. During the 1980s, many newly-emerged nations had fallen into debt. In some cases, their fragile economies were disrupted by civil conflict, while others were weakened by the collapse in the price of their exports. Debts attracted huge loans which had to be repaid on a regular basis. Meanwhile, in the rich nations the proliferation of IT and digitisation meant that viable profits could be made increasingly easily from the mere circulation of money, rather than its transfer into goods and services.[20] For poor and developing states, this meant that capital became disconnected from social relationships. In the past, obligation and trust had to be established between borrower and lender as an essential element of dealing. Now, as borrowers, developing states found themselves increasingly shut out from, or let down by, the international lending system. Wealth had become more mobile, but borrowers were no longer linked to lenders. New investment policies meant that it was becoming increasingly unlikely that capital would move any longer 'from where it is concentrated and politically and strategically safer, to where it is scarce and subject to political and strategic risks'.[21] In the late 1980s, John Reed, the chairman of Citicorp, one of the world's largest banking corporations, confirmed that 'the Third World' had become 'unbankable', and that, with the exception of the stronger Asian economies, the global economy would be increasingly a phenomenon of the northern hemisphere.[22]

The combination of loan-repayment obligations and the diminishing value of state resources removed executive power from governments. Whereas during the Cold War developing states in Latin America, Africa and Asia could manipulate the competing superpowers and extract favourable deals, now the situation was reversed. Particularly in Sub-Saharan Africa, the indebtedness of poor states gave international lenders and the international non-governmental organisations that acted for them enormous leverage. National institutions such as trade unions, parliaments and the media were supplanted by international influences. Transnational corporations, the international media, the global currency market and international development agencies began to inflict their individual prescriptions on client governments. Even the most intimate responsibilities of a state – the management of law and order, welfare, education and health – were now subjected to international scrutiny.[23] Debt reduction, which might have redressed the balance in favour of weakened governments, made no real progress as there was still a strong conditional linkage between reduction and the imposition of apparently 'sound' policies.

The end of the Cold War acted against the Sub-Saharan African states in their search for foreign investment. The priority for international lenders was to rebuild the Central and Eastern European states, and this diverted money away from the immediate needs of developing countries. The old resource-based economies in Sub-Saharan Africa were now under severe pressure from more efficient competitors, such as Malaysia and Indonesia. Synthetic substitutes from industrial countries also increased competition. Sub-Saharan African gross domestic product (GDP) decreased, from an average of 14% of most industrialised states in 1960 to between 5% and 8% in 1987.[24]

Above all, it was increasingly possible for communities to see how deprived they were in the global scale of social endowment, and in particular the inequality between the wealth of the rich nations and the wretchedness of the poor. The speed and volume of capital flows from one country to another had no antecedent. Electronic money at the rate of more than a trillion dollars each day passed from one side of the world to another at the click of a mouse, destabilising the economy of one state in favour of a market trend in another. Some felt that a global community which condoned such inequality and left the weakest to the mercies of volatile economies must also expect that the most deprived elements of that society would find a way of striking back.[25]

Migration

In many cases, vulnerable states which had survived in the artificial conditions of the Cold War were now themselves changing. In African countries, the population increased more rapidly after the 1960s with the introduction of foreign medical-development schemes, which eradicated malaria and lowered child-mortality rates. In broad terms, the population in the north African region increased from 280m to 640m in 30 years. In some countries, the increases were more dramatic; in Kenya, for example, the population soared, from 6m to 12m in the same period, and in Côte d'Ivoire from 3m to 12m.[26] Although the population was still largely rural, a greater proportion was becoming urbanised. Eugene Linden has estimated that this global trend will, by 2025, have 61% of the world's population living in cities.[27] The pressures of rural unemployment, environmental damage to their former homelands and climate change spurred their migration to the cities, where expectations of greater opportunity and better services were seldom fulfilled.[28] Urban areas were themselves changing, with the wealthy in their citadels and gated communities, the poor in their ghettos and squatter areas.[29] Some cities had ceased to function as civil societies as families moved outwards to the suburbs, leaving a lawless vacuum behind them. Rampaging inflation, disease, starvation and banditry became normal. Survival depended on self-sufficiency.[30]

Culture

The projection of goods, capital and influence across borders, from one region to another, generated a pervasive cultural by-product. According to Held and McGrew, radio, film, television and the internet exposed people everywhere to the values of other cultures.[31] Combined with the penetration of branded merchandise and the marketing of branded lifestyles, the growing cultural and economic pressures led to, in Benjamin Barber's shorthand description, a 'McWorld' ethos.[32] McWorld stood for the inexorable assault on pre-modern communities and, in a dully insistent manner, dictated a way of living, how to dress and what to eat, as well as business conventions and social mores. Generally, the penetration of 'global values' down to the poorest levels of society weakened already-vulnerable states. Although young people growing up in poor rural areas of Afghanistan, Somalia, Angola and West Africa differed in their outlook and educating influences, they were uniformly confronted by the same global culture. The McWorld lifestyle reached them in varying degrees; in some cases it was actively resisted, but universally it represented a confrontation with traditional values.

Before the assault of consumerism, young people in developing areas had fewer options for survival and tended to endure the hardship of their existence. In most cases, they maintained their identity and self-respect as part of a traditional or a communal structure. Life was brutal, but it could be endured with the help of these structures; above all, there was the extended family, in which the individual had a sense of place, an identity and a degree of support. In some states, the system of paramount chiefs, organised by the outgoing colonial powers, provided controlling structures for the state government. Chiefs and clan elders imposed themselves as a ruling class, which valued age and traditional authority over youth.

The invasion of global culture reached down to these communities and disturbed them. The lyrics and images which assaulted young people arrived via the internet, from public hoardings, cinema screens and radio, telling them that their conservative values were irrelevant. In the bright images of a consumer culture, they saw young people of both sexes presented as heroes, leaders and role models, and certainly not fastened down by communal conventions and family expectations, where youth deferred to age. The same media also told them how very poor they were, and that they were destined to be excluded from the McWorld lifestyle.

Whether negative or positive, reactions to global culture, particularly by young people, were highly exploitable. Images of consumerism told them there were options to their subsistence lifestyle in rural areas, and many migrated towards urban areas or crossed state boundaries searching for something closer to the attractive lifestyle they had seen. In the former communist space, the gradual erosion inflicted by global culture was exacerbated by the visible collapse of a way of life that had been declining for some time. Identity politics provided national and local leaders, such as Slobodan Milosevic in Serbia and Zviad Gamsakhurdia in Georgia, with the opportunity to exploit the outrage and insecurity that arose from change. Although some argue convincingly that identity politics should not be confused with the violent resistance to invasive global cultures, on the street the resulting conflict was very similar.[33]

In West Africa, young people rejecting the communal lifestyle became a rich source of recruits for local gang leaders. In many cases, while they remained within the family their expectations were low and respite from the hardship of outdoor labour came from simple luxuries. But the poverty of subsistence farming meant that there was very little cash for these diversions. When a young person rejected the traditional lifestyle, the overwhelming motives were not uniformly political or ideological, but also stemmed from a personal need to find an alternative to the grind of subsistence living. Observers and retired insurgents speak of the need to 'make a statement'.[34] In the particular case of Sierra Leone, a popular T-shirt logo featured the American rapper Tupac Shakur, whose songs of rebellion and violence struck a chord with the rootless young.[35] Making a statement in this context might involve a gang of armed boys looting an isolated settlement, burning houses and ransacking a bar. Discontent was widespread, and this energy could be harnessed by the insurgent. The status quo was increasingly threatened; young people had always been inherently lawless and political regimes inherently unjust, but from another world, the nagging lyrics of the rapper helped to make it all seem unbearable.

The cultural attack also came in the form of the television image. Satellite communications meant that local leaders who physically opposed government forces could be interviewed from their rural bases and their faces beamed on to television screens throughout the world. Radio interviewing via insurgents' telephone systems removed the need for the foreign correspondent to be in the same wilderness location as the interviewee. Stations like the BBC World Service and Voice of America were respected in the crisis zones to which they broadcast, and international correspondents in English-language services were vested with a towering stature and credibility that local politicians seldom enjoyed. When these media deities interviewed local military leaders who opposed the government, they conferred on them a statesman-like aura that exaggerated their real significance. Interviewing opponents on an equal footing to national leaders was an acceptable device in rich, safe countries, but in a weakening state, it elevated local war leaders, even warlords and road bandits, to a political importance they neither understood nor deserved. Popular, democratically-elected leaders could cope with competition, but weak and un-popular governments had little capacity to deal with a free media operating intrusively from another region.

Conclusion

Three main conclusions emerge from this chapter: globalisation made weak governments weaker; the insurgent forces that op-posed them became stronger; and new priorities changed the insurgents' *modus operandi*.

No attempt has been made in this assessment to explain how beleaguered governments were also, in varying degrees, corrupt, despotic and undemocratically empowered, and failed to sustain their populations, or a particular community.[36] These failings have not been greatly changed by globalisation.

In the past, an outgoing colonial government handed over controlling structures that could be used to strengthen a ruler's hold over the state. These included a monopoly over the move-ment of cargoes and resources, electronic communications and the accumulation of wealth from the state's natural resources. For an authoritarian regime, controlling these assets sometimes made up for a debilitating lack of competence and legitimacy. The intrusion of technical advances, new means of communications and the impact of a less regulated global economy gradually eroded these monopolies. It became increasingly difficult to control access to resources in wilderness areas, and the movement of these cargoes on to international highways. On another front, traditional or communal social structures, which also acted as controlling devices, were being made to seem irrelevant by imported mores that favoured youth over age. In many governments, there was less cash available for security. After the Cold War, a universal downturn in defence spending led to donor reluctance to fund military forces. States became too poor to pay their armed forces and police. Consequently, some began to work full time growing their own food, and even using their service weapons to extort from local people. This resulted in a shift of power away from the state and into the hands of local commanders, and diminished the responsiveness of the state's armed forces. It became hard to react to a crisis when troops or the local police were busy providing for themselves. As a result, borders were left unmanned and the government's writ shrank to the capital.

For the same reasons that governments became weaker, anti-government forces grew stronger. Eroding monopolies of power within the state gave the insurgent international freedom of movement, association and communication. The demobilisation of Europe's military stocks lowered the price of weapons and war materiel on the international market. Above all, insurgents were immensely richer than before, trading natural resources as well as farmed products directly on to international markets, and in much greater quantities. The invasion of a global culture became their recruiting sergeant, eroding the traditional social structures that had been the controlling devices of a weak government.

These developments also changed the survival strategies of the insurgent. The Cold War insurgent had relied on the local population for logistic supplies, intelligence, concealment and funds. Mao's success as an insurgent leader depended on cultivating a positive relationship with the local population so that, when events turned against him, his forces could return to the people and hide. The movement that lost the support of the population would ultimately fail. But in the post-Cold War world, the trend was moving away from a 'people's war' strategy. The insurgent now needed to secure sources of supply and the facilities to move them on to the international markets. Military objectives became mining areas, plantations and game reserves, and the transport arteries that connected them to air and sea ports. The profits from stripping the state's resources and trading them on to the international market were so enormous that they, rather than any political intent, became the reason for war.[37] The principles of survival and success had altered; popular support was no longer an essential requirement for the military activities associated with looting and the exploitation of a state's resources. Some insurgent forces now used the local population manipulatively, as shields against attack by intervention forces and to attract relief convoys, not for aid purposes but to become part of their logistic resources. A warlord surrounded himself with ethnically-similar communities to create a secure environment for his assets, while hostile groups would be displaced or exterminated. Internationally-provided food and water became the levers of extortion and humanitarian codes of conduct were abandoned.

Chapter 2

The Refinement of Violence

A major consequence of global change is the imposition of uniformity. Technical developments, ideas and cultural fashion are spread without discrimination, so that the traveller from one region recognises the same references and symbols in another. The logic of these developments should be that a corresponding uniformity imposes itself on insurgent forces. But this is not the case: their *modus operandi* and organisations are disparate, so that in their purpose and military approach they bear little similarity to each other. There are evidently other, more immediate influences shaping insurgent forces. This chapter identifies some of these pressures, and explains how they help to define insurgents. The most influential local conditions are the strength of the opposing forces, the environment (referring to terrain, the level of urbanisation and demography), the cultural approach to violence, and the nature of the leadership.

Opposing forces

The strength and effectiveness of opposing forces shape the insurgents' tactical priorities, and each government's counter-strategy is different. The strongest governments, and therefore the ones most difficult for the insurgent to operate against, are formidable because they have a high degree of popular support and legitimacy, as well as being militarily strong. But democratic legitimacy and popularity have to be complemented by secure national borders and friendly and cooperative neighbouring states. Israel is militarily strong in relation to the opposing Palestinian insurgent forces, but the proximity of intensely hostile populations and neighbouring states which support the Palestinian cause considerably diminishes the advantages of being strong in such a narrow sense. The Palestinian insurgents move, attack and survive devastating counter-efforts time after time because they receive assistance at every level.

As governments become more popular and democratically mature, they also become vulnerable, regardless of their military strength. The checks and devices which ensure government account-ability and the population's individual freedom also become the instruments of the insurgent. Freedom of association, the right to strike and to demonstrate, a free media, access to information, the laws of privacy and habeas corpus, are all essential for democracy, but they also provide operating freedom for the terrorist. A state also becomes vulnerable as it grows richer and its population con-centrates in urban areas, which rely on sophisticated public services. It becomes increasingly difficult to secure these services and prevent fears that they can be threatened.[1] Public concern can be manipu-lated in regard to the safety of public transport and public areas, and attendance at recreational events and state occasions. In high-density, high-rise urban areas, the interruption of services, power, water, refuse collection, even the blockage of a single traffic artery – all can quickly make life seem unbearable to thousands of citizens.

A dangerous insurgency, as opposed to a fringe terrorist group in the animal-rights category, usually has a legitimate griev-ance or cause. A successful counter-strategy requires a government that is politically strong enough to change direction in order to remove the pressure of the grievance, and at the same time hopefully remove a substantial element of popular support from the insurgent.[2] But the ability of the state to mount an effective counter-insurgent campaign is not always commensurate with its democratic maturity and wealth. In addition to these attributes, experience is an important factor. An undemocratic regime, which nevertheless has a professional and experienced counter-insur-gency organisation, may be able to resist an insurgency and therefore survive longer than a similar regime which does not. In British Cold War experience, a successful counter-insurgency organisation had to involve all the instruments of governance, not just the military and the police. This meant a host of civil actors, including public relations, the media, urban administration, education and local authorities, was involved in the counter-strategy, in addition to the state's security forces.[3]

The strength and skill of the government forces are the most powerful determinants of an insurgent campaign. Each state reacts differently in these circumstances. The variables which influence a government's response are: the degree of support from global organisations, regional security, domestic legitimacy, popular support, democratic accountability, individual rights, the effectiveness of government ministries, political strength and flexibility, quality of operational leadership and direction, the experience and professionalism of the security forces and the cooperation of civil authorities. With so many variables influencing their success and failure, each government's approach is different, and consequently dictates different manifestations of insurgent organisation.

The environment

The territory in which an insurgent chooses to operate is dictated in most cases by the ambitions of the movement. A faction that seeks to loot and sell natural resources will wish to be where these items are, and to hold the exit routes for their removal. A faction that seeks to overthrow a political regime will move in different operational areas. In the final stages of the campaign, the more politically-motivated insurgents would hope to be near the centres of power within the state. However, until they are strong enough to hold on to these key facilities, they will have to stay closer to their logistic bases and their sources of popular support. In northern Sri Lanka, Jaffna is the traditional administrative centre for the secessionist Tamil territory. Although the Liberation Tigers of Tamil Eelam (LTTE) have on several occasions felt strong enough to invest Jaffna, they have not held it continuously. In Angola, the Cold War version of the National Union for the Total Independence of Angola (UNITA), massively supported by the US and South Africa, established its enclaves around rural population centres at Jamba. After the Cold War, UNITA lost its base at Jamba and its sources of external support. Consequently, its military objectives changed from the control of people and territory to the control of resources, and it moved northwards into new areas.

In many states, the pace of urbanisation and the simultaneous development of rural communications force insurgents into urban areas. There are some tactical advantages for insurgents in the city. Unregulated urbanisation creates sprawling townships, which are no-go areas even for the most militarily-powerful regimes. No amount of surveillance and firepower can distinguish the urban guerrilla from the mass of people among whom they move and operate. In poor, overcrowded areas there is a general lawlessness and hostility towards the government and its security forces which favours the insurgent. In times of hardship and unrest, a crowd of several hundred can gather in seconds in a high-density living area.[4] In addition, the centre of power is close at hand. Government buildings, the air terminal, docks, power stations, communication masts and broadcasting facilities are all within striking distance. However, the promiscuity of the township population allows the government to infiltrate urban subversive groups with great facility. To survive against a well-organised counter-strategy, an urban insurgency usually organises itself into smaller groups, or cells, which exist separately and move, not overtly as armed bands, but with the appearance of unarmed civilians. At the lowest level, the insurgent fighters are urban dwellers themselves, who can pass for city people and also operate with an innate street sense. The nature of built-up areas also dictates the character of the violence. It is hard to regroup small, urban-based cells into an effective military unit without detection. But the availability of explosive materials, and the vehicles to carry them in large quantities, make it easier to attack individuals and installations with the proxy bomb, as in the massive truck-bomb attacks in Beirut in 1983, and Nairobi in 1998.[5]

Insurgent forces operate in rural areas because they have failed to gain a foothold in the city, or because their objectives are better served in the countryside. In either case, the strength of government forces, in particular their mobility and firepower, has a much greater bearing on the insurgent force. A strong government opposition can control the countryside and isolate the insurgent. Freedom of movement becomes a major concern for both parties. Government forces with powerful military assets should be able to enjoy freedom of movement and, as far as possible, will strive to reduce it for the insurgent. The use of roadblocks, surveillance and random stop-and-search operations compels the weaker insurgent to move clandestinely and split into smaller groups. For the insurgent, concentrating forces for an attack becomes a problem, requiring elaborate subterfuge and even rehearsal before the operation is launched. Weapons may have to be moved clandestinely and linked to crews close to the objective. After the attack, the insurgent forces must disperse and prepare to survive or evade retaliatory search-and-destroy operations by government troops.

Hiding is becoming more and more difficult in rural areas. In the past, the wilderness acted as a leveller. The mountainous deserts of Central Asia, the rainforests and the bush have been a refuge for the insurgent, where numbers and heavy weapons count less. But by the 1990s, better vehicles, aircraft, helicopters, long-range weapons and a shrinking wilderness enabled a well-equipped military force to find and destroy the insurgent more easily.[6] In December 2001, it was safer for the defeated Taliban and al-Qaeda fighters to stay among crowds of displaced people than to flee to remote, isolated areas, where their presence identified them as targets.

Against a government too weak to move and fight beyond the edge of the capital, many of the limitations of rural areas are reversed in favour of the insurgent. In this situation, insurgent forces move boldly in large armed bands without fear of opposition. The need for elaborate planning and clandestine regrouping is removed and attacks can be crude affairs, sometimes conducted without subterfuge or much competence. Insurgent forces mirror the characteristics of their opposition; against a weak and poorly-organised government, there is little incentive for military professionalism. In the absence of governance in rural areas, insurgents fill the vacuum by creating their own state within a state. In elaborate versions of a rural no-go area, there will be a *de facto* administration, insurgent currency, police, a hospital, a radio station, a newspaper, a guest house for visitors and even bars and night-clubs.[7]

Each insurgency is therefore distinguished by the ground on which it fights: an urban-based insurgency has a different operational appearance from its rural counterpart. In the city, the proxy bomb and the riotous crowd lead the attack, whereas in rural areas the importance of distance and range call for a different fighting approach. Weapon categories, including artillery and mortars, have more significance in rural areas, and their possession influences the conduct of the campaign on both sides to a much greater extent than in the city.

Different cultures of violence

The human factor in the success or failure of an insurgency is overwhelming, and introduces a strong variable between one insurgent force and another. If a successful insurgent movement is empowered by a population, the cultural influences of that society dictate different approaches to violence and popular mobilisation.

The dispersal, culture and education of the populations involved in an insurgency vary considerably. Christopher Clapham argues that African insurgents come from widely differing societies. Ethiopian and Rwandan insurgents originate from hierarchical societies with a developed sense of statehood, while in Somalia faction fighters are first of all clansmen, with powerful ties to family and a strong belief in their own community, which confront the concept of a state. The Sudanese insurgent also comes from a stateless society.[8] In Liberia, the indigenous communities that provided the fighters in the 1990s' conflict were divided into 16 ethnically different groups straddling the borders of different states. This gave the National Patriotic Front of Liberia (NPFL) logistical flexibility and a wider area from which to extract natural resources, while remaining surrounded by a supportive host population.[9]

Migration and the degree of adaptation of rural societies to urban areas introduce a further variable. Within a lifetime, migrants to the city take on the values and instincts of urban dwellers, at the same time assimilating their culture of violence. The Tupamaros of the Uruguayan grasslands became a highly-skilled urban guerrilla movement in Montevideo in the 1960s, using even the sewers with great facility.[10] More recently, intolerable circumstances in some developing states and a growing global labour market have increased the number of diaspora populations. Each diaspora is distinct, but for the purposes of sustaining an insurgency, communities abroad that have wealth and are split as families (part abroad and part remaining in the area controlled by the insurgent) are vulnerable to extortion. In particular, the split family allows the faraway insurgent organisation a degree of leverage on the wealth-producing element. Cheaper travel and proliferating communications have also increased the significance of the diaspora population as a logistic entrepôt, as well as a source of international agents.

In general, the populations from each continent, Europe, Sub-Saharan Africa and Central Asia, have developed differently in their approach to violence. The horse-riding inhabitants of the Central Asian grasslands lived constantly on practical necessities and skills that were entirely transferable to the conduct of violence:

> in their management of animals they showed a matter-of-factness in mustering, droving, culling, slaughter for food – that taught direct lessons about how masses of people on foot, even inferior cavalry men, could be harried, outflanked, cornered and eventually killed without risk ... When a horse horde closed in for a kill, it slaughtered without compunction. There was absolutely no hint of ritual or ceremony ... they fought to win – quickly, completely and quite unheroically. Eschewal of heroic display was, indeed, almost a rule.[11]

The raider instinct lives on despite the uniformity of modern weapons and urbanisation. In societies that are more regulated by conflict than by the rule of law, disputes lead to violence, internal rivalries and blood feuds on matters of day-to-day survival, such as access to water and grazing.[12]

The Sub-Saharan African stereotype of the relationship of culture to violence can be illustrated at one level by the Zulu nation and its large fighting units. But at a lower level, the nature of violence is not always conditioned by the practicalities of survival, and spiritual concerns could be more significant. During the uprising of the Holy Spirit Movement (HSM) in Uganda in the 1980s, Alice Lakwena's emphasis on a spiritual approach to conflict resulted in crude tactics, an absolute reliance on the magical protective powers of her spiritual credo and a military organisation that became too unwieldy to control without a more competent officer cadre.[13] The lesson for insurgent forces driven by spiritual concerns was that they could be defeated by a more rigorously-trained and practically-organised military unit. The trench provided better protection for the temporal being than holy ointment. The spiritual influence among insurgent movements extends to West Africa, where a similar concern for witchcraft over military practicalities manifests itself in Liberia, and in neighbouring Sierra Leone.[14]

In Europe, the imposition of the state-regulated use of violence cut across the cultural distinctions of each community and their individual ways of fighting. The institutionalisation of violence and the emergence of the regiment required a similar uniformity of discipline and approach as that which Shaka's Zulu units had achieved from a separate cultural heritage.[15] Individual foot-soldiers were required to abandon their natural instincts for personal gain and survival, and submit themselves to a collective discipline and the higher political ambitions of the state. Another dimension of European violence was the organisation of resistance movements, which in the Balkans considerably predates the German occupation of the Second World War. Such movements re-emerged in the 1990s as a powerful cultural determinant of the war aims and methodology of the factions in the former Yugoslavia.[16]

The differences between populations, their dispersal, culture, wealth and education, are therefore an important variable. In particular, these influences dictate different approaches towards violence, and distinguish one insurgency from another.

Leadership

Some attributes of leadership are inherited, and some develop under the influence of circumstances and through the efforts of the individual concerned. In both cases, leadership is an important determinant of an insurgent movement's success and its operating style. A leader's influence is particularly important when they have the freedom to choose how they are to operate, and contributes heavily towards success or extinction.[17] A hugely powerful personality will grow in stature to become a head of state or even an international statesman, as in the case of Nelson Mandela. A lesser individual fails to rise beyond operational command, and those in the lowest stratum may degenerate into road bandits.

The leader's ethnicity and formative years are fundamental. Some leaders are born, raised and educated within the community they are destined to lead as insurgents. LTTE leader Velupillai Prabhakaran is Jaffna-born, and spent his early years in Velvetti-turai, 'a small and closely knit coastal town of some 10,000 Tamils'.[18] By contrast Charles Taylor, a Liberian-American by birth, enjoyed a privileged childhood among the Monrovia elite. With an

American higher education he was altogether distinct from the indigenous Liberians, who came from poor rural communities and were the foot-soldiers of the NPFL.[19]

In the dangerous and fugitive circumstances of insurgency, there is little scope for leadership training: the inherited characteristics of a movement's leader are crucial, and include almost everything in his curriculum vitae on the day he chooses to be an insurgent. There are, however, important exceptions to this rule. During the Cold War, when the ideological struggle between East and West reached down to insurgent movements, a lucky minority of young leaders went overseas for special training. Candidates were spotted and contacted for this purpose, depending on their determination to be noticed by Soviet and Chinese talent scouts. Once chosen, some attended schools in China, Russia, Cuba, Eastern Europe and later in Libya, where their most important experience was often to meet other future leaders. Revolutionary United Front (RUF) leader Foday Sankoh met Charles Taylor in Libya when both were guests of President Muammar Gaddafi at the Matabh Ideological Centre in Tripoli in the late 1980s. [20] Foreign training also introduced a strong element of Marxist ideology into revolutionary manifestos.

In a dangerously competitive environment, only the strongest survived to become the head of a movement. The leaders considered in this paper have three survival characteristics: charm, absolute ruthlessness and a keen instinct for spotting challenges to their authority from within. The leader of an insurgent movement usually has no qualms in organising the assassination of subordinates, or a close friend who might threaten his position. If these can be regarded as the common requirements for attaining the highest rank in an insurgent movement, the distinguishing feature is therefore the degree of ambition and the quality of vision, beyond the essentials for survival.

Individual ambitions vary a great deal. At the highest end of the scale, Osama bin Laden has a global vision of his cause. At the opposite end, John Garang, leader of the Sudan People's Liberation Army (SPLA), is ostensibly fighting for the autonomy of southern Sudan, but increasingly divides his time between his villa at Karin, in a fashionable suburb of Nairobi, and his fighting units in the field.

Garang's critics in Kenya argue that the SPLA profits more from continuing the war in southern Sudan than it would from its cessation, and Garang has already achieved his personal ambition of a villa and an air-conditioned jeep. Although personal integrity does not appear to be a *sine qua non* for individual success in an insurgent organisation, it does have an interesting correlation to ambitious long-term goals. At the high end of the scale of vision and ambition, both bin Laden and Prabhakaran live in monastic austerity and eschew the marble-villa lifestyle, whereas at the lower end of the scale, Sankoh, Taylor and Garang seem to relish it.

A leader's operational intent also varies considerably. Clapham identifies four categories of intent: *liberation insurgencies*, which set out to achieve independence from colonial or minority rule, as in Namibia or South Africa; *separatist insurgencies*, which champion a particular ethnicity or region within a state, such as the SPLA in southern Sudan; *reform insurgencies*, which seek to replace an existing national government that at best has failed to exercise its writ and responsibilities; and finally *warlord insurgencies*, which challenge the existing regime in order to maintain a sub-state within the state or, in the case of Taylor and Aideed in Somalia, replace an essentially rapacious regime with their own, equally rapacious leadership. David Keen adds a fifth category, whereby local war leaders maintain an environment of violence in order to extort profits.[21] These categories emphasise the variety of possible long-term objectives.

Despite the uniformity of each leader's survival qualities and, in some cases, the similarity in inspirational education, the overriding variable element lies in their vision, ambitions and selection of long-term objectives. Whether by heredity or environment, these qualities are already in the behaviour and personality of future leaders when they become insurgents.

Conclusion

Although globalisation tended to impose a sense of uniformity on many visible aspects of life between regions and cultures, it failed to achieve the same regularity between the insurgencies that flourished after the Cold War. The impact of global change was largely overridden by the more immediate influences of territory, culture, leadership and, above all, the nature of the opposing forces.

Chapter 3

The Classification of Insurgent Forces

During the Cold War and in the 1990s, academics, peace negotiators and security forces were animated by different aspects of terrorism and insurgency, and therefore created different orders of insurgent types. Although individually valid, these are inconsistent as instruments of analysis. Clapham's four categories referred to in the previous chapter – liberation, separatist, reform and warlord – explain insurgents' aspirations, but not their manifestations.[1] The separatist movement in Tigray, with its fundamentalist Marxist ideology and conventional tactics, fighting in trench systems like those at Flanders in 1914–18, is far removed in its manifestation from the SPLA in southern Sudan, which is also by intent separatist. Clapham's classification was preceded by O'Neill's, which 18 years previously had identified seven national insurgent types that could be applied globally: anarchist, egalitarian, traditionalist, pluralist, separatist, reformist and preservationist.[2]

Although the lists differ, Clapham and O'Neill, and later the British Ministry of Defence, all take the same approach, which is to describe the apparent aspirations of the insurgents, and not their physical manifestation. In the 1990s, categorisation by aspiration became increasingly invalid. Keen's work on the economic reasons for inciting and prolonging civil violence, and the associated literature, indicate that a movement's apparent political intent in many cases is not necessarily its real motivation for the conduct of violence.[3] The rhetoric of insurgency is misleading. Although the SPLA has strong claims to be regarded as a separatist or secessionist movement, reports from Western observers, and the conduct of the movement itself, call this definition into question.[4] The SPLA is accused of profiting from the violence in southern Sudan, and has created an echelon of its organisation to attract relief, which routinely becomes the logistic support for the armed element of the insurgent force.[5] It is not helpful to place the SPLA and the Tigray People's Liberation Front in the same category, if that also implies that they are similar movements and therefore should be regarded and approached in the same manner.

Lawrence Freedman has categorised the al-Qaeda phenomenon as 'super terrorism', at the same time placing all other movements under the collective heading of 'normal terrorism'. Freedman defined the 'super terrorist' by the statistics and techniques of its tactical successes: a 'super terrorist' may rely on 'chemical and biological, or even nuclear weapons [to] cause casualties in the low thousands and upwards'.[6] There are problems with disengaging al-Qaeda from the wider array of insurgent movements, some of which have similar characteristics. Those in the 'normal category' vary considerably; some, like the LTTE, are close to al-Qaeda in organisation and global reach, while others such as the RUF have no similarity. There is also a randomness about relying completely on the significance of the kill-score; until a movement inflicts a 1,000-casualty incident, it does not appear in the list of 'super terrorists'. Nevertheless, al-Qaeda's involvement in efforts to destroy the World Trade Center in 1993, and its plans to organise the destruction of up to 4,000 passengers and 11 aircraft in the Pacific region, should have put it in a separate category eight years before the attack on the World Trade Center in 2001.[7] But until fate determined that an attempt was successful, the organisation was classified as 'normal'. After its success nothing about al-Qaeda changed except the casualty statistics. Jonathan Stevenson also disengages al-Qaeda from the global order of insurgent forces, distinguishing them as 'new terrorists', and previous movements as 'old terrorists'. Old terrorists, he says, are 'constrained by nationalist or irredentist goals, a Palestinian state, a united Ireland, that are negotiable … they take responsibility for their acts in order to make it clear that bloodletting will stop when their demands are met'. Old terrorists want to bargain; new terrorists express wrath and cripple their enemy with a sense of absolutism that allows for no negotiation.[8]

Stevenson's and Freedman's distinctions both refer to different facets of the same object. The problem for the doctrine writer and contingency planner is that there are too many random and unrelated classifications of insurgency (or terrorism) to choose from. Each might have a valid definition of a particular characteristic, but the sum does not present a coherent explanation of the whole.

The central proposition of this paper is that global change has widened the span of insurgent forces, so that there are now at least four distinct categories. The strategic environment has shifted, and a more precise classification of insurgency is needed which must comprise the insurgent's practical manifestation, as well as the rhetoric of its motives and aspirations.

The four categories which emerge in this analysis are: Lumpen, Clan, Popular and Global. Each category is explained as a stereotype or model that is made up of a number of facets, including motivation, strength of opposition, environment, leadership, organisation, recruitment, tactics and international reach. By considering these traits together and creating models, it becomes possible to overcome some of the contradictions that arise in a classification that relies on a single characteristic. The corollary to this finding is that a single-fix prescription for counter-insurgent doctrine is not valid.[9] Strategies will have to be nuanced and systemic, and have a stronger political imperative beyond the narrow application of military force.[10]

These models are not prescriptive: successful commanders have an aversion to being confined by doctrine, and low-level operations require an intuitive approach that embraces the idiosyncratic nature of each contingency. This analysis endorses that approach. The categories below are designed to be instruments of assessment, which help to explain the nature of a particular insurgent movement. In reality, an insurgency is more complicated than any model; none fits the parameters of a model precisely, and each has characteristics that spread across more than one type. Despite this weakness, the models explain aspects of behaviour and organisation that determine the nature of an insurgent group. The models are refined by the addition of generic questions about the insurgents' activities as warlords and, at the lowest level, whether the fighters behave as 'soldiers' or 'warriors'.

Lumpen insurgent forces

'Lumpen' is a pejorative expression referring to the rabble elements of an urban population. In the context of insurgency, it has a Marxist dimension to indicate the revolutionary potential of an outcast social group that lies below the proletariat. For the purposes of this model, Lumpen refers to the nature of the fighters, to the cultural sources of their energy and to the lack of sophistication of the movement. The concept and the terminology are not new. Keen describes the syndrome more sympathetically as 'bottom-up economic violence'.[11] The expression 'Lumpen' is used by Ibrahim Abdullah and Patrick Muana to describe the rebellious youth culture of Freetown in the 1940s. [12] In 2001, diplomats and military advisers in West Africa continued to use the term to describe the competence and organisation of a particular type of rebel force. This model develops these informal definitions into a more coherent entity.

Motivation and influences

A Lumpen insurgent force is seldom inspired solely by ideology, and is influenced culturally, even intellectually, at several levels. At the street level, the Lumpen element of the population has historically provided the backbone of the mob. In the 1960s, Martin Oppenheimer identified an under-employed, unemployed and un-employable sub-class, which had no social structures or role to play, and which would 'tend towards the politics of moderation'.[13] Paradoxically, this social group was conservative, even reactionary, in its politics, as long as life seemed bearable. But when their perception of their own circumstances changed and life seemed unbearable, Oppenheimer's Lumpens readily turned to violence and revolution: 'they have nothing to lose, only the world to gain, so why not?'.[14]

Abdullah identifies a similar social stratum in Freetown. In the 1940s, first-generation Freetown Lumpens were city residents, defectively educated, with ill-formed political beliefs. They congregated in social groups at particular venues or *potes* to talk, drink, smoke marijuana and behave in what other groups considered to be an anti-social manner. By the 1970s, pop music and reggae additionally energised them with the lyrics of resistance, which at this stage were derived from the struggle against apartheid. The *pote* culture spread from the suburbs of Freetown to the provincial centres beyond, and attracted young people from other levels of society, who found that its inventive energy had begun to take over the 'cutting edge of the development of the Krio language'.[15] Another level of influence on the Lumpen insurgent force came from the university campus. In the 1960s and 1970s, when students across the world were challenging authority in a wild and exuberant manner, the same energy leached into the Lumpen communities. In Freetown, students joined the *pote*, and in Accra and Monrovia a similar cross-fertilisation was taking place. In Freetown, the discussion was enlivened by the slogans of Marx, Fanon, Castro and Guevara.[16]

At the highest level, the Lumpen insurgency may be influenced by its leadership. However, this source of inspiration tends not to be intellectually developed, original or even strongly influential. Taylor had the benefit of a higher education in the US, as well as training in Libya in 1988. Nevertheless, he failed to develop a credible manifesto before he launched his first military expedition into Nimba county in 1989. By 1994 Taylor, now in his state-within-a-state at Gbarnga, was preparing for a political campaign. This required him to articulate a political concept for his military action. But Taylor's conceptualisation had come as an after-thought, not as an inspirational basis for action. In his headquarters, a huge mural depicted the exploits of the NPFL and its leaders in a primitive style that was directed at the rank and file.[17] However, Taylor's concept for a just society that guaranteed individual security and freedoms did not express itself convincingly beyond his headquarters compound; a few miles down the road towards Monrovia, armed gangs of NPFL fighters continued to harass and extort from the civilian population.[18]

Gibril Foday-Mussa maintains that, in the 1980s, the initial nucleus of revolutionary planners in Freetown earnestly believed in Thomas Sankara's dictum that 'a soldier without a political education is a potential criminal'.[19] However, Libyan impatience led to the introduction of Foday Sankoh, who step by step took over the movement and then agitated for military activation before an ideology had crystallised. Sankoh published a manifesto, 'The Footpath to Democracy', in 1996. The RUF, it maintained, represented a better alternative to the current corrupt government of Sierra Leone. The more articulate political exponents and ideologues became members of the Revolutionary United Front Party (RUFP). However, 'The Footpath to Democracy' was not strictly relevant to the needs of Sierra Leone's deprived communities, and owed a great deal to the manifestos of Mao and Gaddafi. Although the RUF website continued to challenge its international critics, its energy is directed outwards to the world at large, and not towards inspiring the behaviour of RUF fighters. Ideology and the struggle for change are no longer the driving force behind the uprising, and military action comes before the conceptualisation of a motive, rather than stemming from it. Lumpen energy arises from the street, from the volatile Lumpen culture itself and not from an intellectually-developed ideology.

Strength of opposition

A Lumpen insurgency flourishes in a weak state. A stronger government that is more democratically empowered, or simply more competent, will tend to contain and even overcome the symptoms of a Lumpen uprising. In Indonesia and Nigeria, there are strongly Lumpen elements in both urban and rural areas. Although there have been serious lapses of law and order and dangerous rioting, the security forces have been strong enough to limit the effects, and no cohesive movement has emerged. A weaker government, which cannot rise to meet the challenge, may have been debilitated for several reasons. The weakening effects of global change have been explained in Chapter 1. A government is also weakened by its own conduct, its loss of democratic support, its kleptocratic behaviour and its despotic disregard of personal freedoms.

Many weak states suffer from some or all of these problems. The specific conditions that allow a Lumpen uprising to take place and survive for several years are manifested visibly on the ground in the government's failure to enforce its writ. A state that is too poor to pay its police and armed forces loses control of its territory and population. The government's reach is diminished by mutiny and by the armed forces organising their own militias and holding territory on their own account. In Liberia, the Armed Forces of Liberia (AFL) had reduced itself to the status of a faction by 1994.[20] In Sierra Leone, a more serious disintegration and disaffection among government forces took place.[21] The ruling elite may distrust its own armed forces and keep them underpaid and under-resourced, so helping to make them unfit to carry out their function. In the case of Sierra Leone and Liberia, many of the rank and file of the government forces had more in common, culturally and politically, with the rebels than with the metropolitan elite whose security they half-heartedly struggled to maintain.[22]

The conditions which favour a Lumpen uprising manifest themselves gradually. Borders are left unprotected, and large areas beyond the state capital are abandoned by government officials as well as the police and armed forces. There has been no fierce military contest, no destructive fighting. The government is still visible in its capital city, at its international points of entry, at some of its foreign embassies and at the UN. But in its own territories the withdrawal has left a vacuum. In most cases, the initial insurgents need do no more than 'push against a door that is so rotten it falls from its frame'.[23]

Leadership and authority

As suggested in Chapter 2, there is a strong element of chance about the nature of the overall leader of an insurgency, which cannot be reduced to fit a stereotypical model. Taylor organised the Lumpen constituents of the NPFL, but was far from being a Lumpen himself. Below the highest level of command, however, the unit leaders tend to relate more strongly to the character of the insurgency and the conditions from which it has succeeded. In a Lumpen insurgent force, the top leader may be a random quantity, but his lieutenants will be a product of the culture that empowers the movement. This section describes the attributes of the Lumpen lieutenant.

Although a Lumpen insurgent force may be energised by an urban culture, its military activities take place largely, though not entirely, in rural areas. In the wilderness, a commander operates in a social vacuum because, most of the time, he is alone in the bush with his followers, and there are no structures or institutions to challenge or even question their behaviour. He encounters no resistance, and therefore sets his own rules. His power is not derived from his rank within the structure of a force, but by his formidable presence. Because this power is rooted so superficially, he has to maintain a dominant position as leader of the group in a very physical manner, by his appearance, his behaviour and his immediate confrontation of dissent. In his isolation, a unit commander may suffer from personality distortions. Surrounded by doting followers, his utterances take on a messianic quality, and his self-belief becomes inexhaustible. His appearance and behaviour are intended to convey a frightening sense of authority and power to his followers. His self-importance becomes even more overwhelming when his image and statements are broadcast by the international media. Sankoh made predictive statements about himself which greatly enhanced his standing in the RUF (especially when some of them turned out to be correct).[24] His beard and smock were derived from the nineteenth-century Tenmeh resistance hero Bai Bureh, whose pictures show a similar appearance.[25]

In the case of the RUF, the commanders at unit level changed as the insurgency developed. Although some of the top leadership remained, the educated element below was replaced by cadres from a different background. The later arrivals had a strong street sense and could grapple with convoluted situations, but they were in many cases illiterate. Issa Sesay, who replaced Sankoh, fits the Lumpen leadership stereotype. Although he was an able field commander, decisive, brutal and ruthless in dealing with rivals, he needed to have a reader with him in his headquarters. His long-term ambitions were venal: a Suzuki jeep, constant access to sources of wealth and several villas near Freetown.[26]

A foreign diplomat in Freetown describes a meeting with a commander of the Armed Forces Revolutionary Council (AFRC), which illustrates the outward display of formidable authority:

Colonel 'Savage' by this time had a comparatively well established unit. At the meeting point the first members of his faction to appear from the bush were the porters who carried his shelter, bedding, cooking utensils as well as his personal effects. They were accompanied by some of his wives. Next to appear were his warriors, young men and boys holding automatic weapons. Colonel 'Savage's' enforcers moved close beside him and carried sticks which they used to switch the warriors and to indicate the positions to which they should move.

At the meeting 'Savage' wore heavy, wrap-around, dark glasses and was accompanied by an interpreter. During the discussion he sat back in his chair and looked away from us, indicating by his posture that he was extremely bored by the whole affair. He spoke throughout via the interpreter, although it was clear that he followed the English version.[27]

Organisation of the movement

A Lumpen force is characterised by its weak or informal organisation. Despite the appearance of a vertical structure, with 'brigades', 'battalions' and staff departments for intelligence, logistics and civil liaison, the reality does not live up to the titles. A Lumpen force is horizontally structured. The standard independent unit is sometimes referred to as a 'battalion', but this does not so much indicate its strength, which can vary considerably, as its independent status. Several 'battalions' comprise a 'brigade'. Within the RUF, Abdullah identifies the informal categories of commanders and warriors as: vanguards (leaders and reconnaissance), special forces, *salon wosus* or the rank and file, standbys (captives under training), and recruits.[28] Females in the RUF were mostly recruited by capture and grouped in the Combat Wives Unit, where they acted as bodyguards and civil controllers.[29]

In the West Side Boys, a group mainly comprising former soldiers, 'battalions' did not rely on the 'brigade' for sustainment except in an important operation, when they might receive reinforcements and extra firepower. The independence of each 'battalion' was symbolised by having its own generator, TV set, medical staff and padre. The West Side Boys did not care about the welfare or opinion of the local civil community, and would routinely intercept public transport and strip passengers of their possessions.[30]

Lumpen forces are, in organisational terms, the manifestation of a junior NCO's view of a military unit. The nomenclature and the life-regulating parades of a regular force battalion are recognisable, but only superficially similar. This is due in many cases to the fact that the unit organisations are indeed designed by junior NCOs, who have deserted from the government's security forces. Because the structure is, despite its titles, informal and horizontal, the control of sub-units is inconsistent and 'battalions' may skirmish with each other over loot and prize objectives. A 'brigade' HQ may appear to have staff departments with Western military-style titles, but a local *modus operandi* tends to take over in the bush. Intelligence may be gathered by children moving ahead of the main body or by word of mouth. Besides the provision of food and ammunition, logistics includes the commandeering of civilian transport to move fighters from one area to another. This may be achieved by hijack, or in some cases by 'enforced borrowing' from international agencies working in the same area.

At lower levels, discipline is extremely harsh. In a 'battalion', the enforcement of discipline has to be continuous and immediate to prevent the structure from falling apart. A 'battalion' may parade each morning before its patrols move out. During these parades, offenders are publicly punished. Offences include rape, desertion, cowardice during combat, loss of weapons and insubordination. Offenders may be beaten with sticks or rubber whips and kept in lock-ups underground. A 'battalion' commander may even be punished by his 'brigade' commander. The brutality of the system is accepted and a punished warrior continues to function after punishment.[31] Drugs and alcohol may be used as an additional controlling device. Some observers maintain that child soldiers and warriors are encouraged to form a dependency, which intensifies a need for drug rewards and becomes a controlling mechanism. Drugs may also give the user courage. The distribution of drugs and alcohol follows the rank hierarchy. Locally-made alcohol and marijuana are for warriors, and cocaine and heroine are reserved mainly for senior officers and are found and used closer to the main logistic arteries. In the case of the RUF, officer-category drugs are usually imported from Nigeria.[32]

At the warrior level, living in a conflict area beyond the protection of an armed band is dangerous and hard, and so supporting the group and its leader is a matter of survival. Unless they carry weapons, civilians are the most vulnerable and can be routinely robbed and raped by any passing gang or 'battalion'. Lumpen units maintain a rapacious attitude towards the civil population. This disregard for local communities was emphasised in the case of the RUF's commander Sesay, who in 2001 had no public radio and was careless of his relations with the local people, and as a result was an unknown personality. The RUF's newspaper, *The Lion*, was also a poor effort, printed on A4 paper in a format which was frequently spoofed and ridiculed by government propaganda versions.[33]

In addition to the need for survival, a warrior may feel a strong sense of identity as part of an armed group. This may manifest itself in the wearing of similar articles of clothing, or similar colours or headgear.[34] After an attack, the assaulting group may be told to disperse into the captured area for 24 hours to plunder, after which the group will reassemble and there will be no more looting. In the RUF, a warrior is expected to hand over valuable objects to his seniors, but may keep or consume lesser items. In some 'battalions', rape is heavily punished; in others, it is condoned in certain circumstances.[35]

At a wider level of organisation, a Lumpen movement, operating from a weak state and derived from a comparatively small population, is unlikely to have a developed interest in operations overseas, except commercially. Although Liberian and Sierra Leonean communities live in Europe and adjacent West African states, as a diaspora they do not support insurgent movements. Lumpen movements 'think globally' for all the reasons Mark Duffield identifies, but in the scale of insurgent movements around the world, this dimension of their activities is relatively undeveloped.[36] A Lumpen movement does not typically have a military reach overseas, and is unlikely to bomb, assassinate or extort beyond the host state. Although a Lumpen force will trade its resources outwards on to the international markets, bank, move its funds, import weapons and purchase medical supplies, this does not imply a well-developed overseas commercial wing. In many cases, the intermediary transactions between Lumpens and the markets are done by foreign traders, who are already established in the host state. Bank accounts may be held in the names of relatives based overseas, but this does not amount to an overseas operational presence.

Operating methods

A Lumpen force's operations are usually a reliable indicator of its real long-term motivations. A force which is drawing closer to the capital city is more likely to be concerned with overthrowing or influencing the incumbent regime, whereas a force that occupies areas holding valuable resources may have a stronger interest in their removal and sale. A Lumpen force operates mostly at 'battalion' level, though from time to time larger operations are mounted to secure a major objective, or for political reasons.[37] However, 'battalion'-level operations generally have the purpose of seizing supplies that guarantee the survival of the group.

Although a 'battalion'-level operation may be reconnoitred in a clandestine manner, the plan is usually simple. Women and children from the 'battalion' will approach the objective, usually a village with a food surplus, and search for armed men from the opposing forces. If the objective is strongly held, the 'battalion' may not attack. Some effort will be made to surprise the defenders by use of darkness, concealment or subterfuge. The main body usually approaches along the axis of an obvious track and seldom subdivides into flanking units. An escape route is left open for armed defenders to use.

Combat during the attack has a ritualistic quality. The attackers are unlikely to be carrying much ammunition, and they therefore hope that, at the sound of gunfire, the armed defenders will flee without forcing a contest. There are unlikely to be many casualties caused by warriors firing on opposing warriors. International military training staff in Sierra Leone report that a high number of warriors close their eyes as they press the trigger, and international agencies involved in medical care confirm that, in conflict areas where 'battalion' combat takes place, there are few casualties caused by warrior-on-warrior shooting, as opposed to unarmed civilians with gunshot wounds.[38] Most warrior casualties are from fever and waterborne diseases.

A miscalculated attack can have serious consequences. If the attackers run out of ammunition before the defenders have left, they will withdraw without taking their objective. This leaves them greatly weakened and vulnerable. After a failed attack they will be without small-arms ammunition or food and cannot become effective again as a combat unit until they have successfully replenished their stocks, which will be much harder without ammunition.

After an objective is taken, a 'battalion' may remain in the area as a garrison. The group coalesces around its commander, who will be close to his radio communications. The civilians who remain in the area will continue to live on what is left of their resources. The occupying 'battalion' will regulate traffic through the area by setting up road blocks. Local civilians are expected to inform the 'battalion' of any unusual occurrence or movement. Each household will be required to provide labour and rations to the garrison in its area and, during a long insurgency, a subjugated community tends to develop a weary acceptance of these obligations.

A battalion moving into a new area will recruit wherever possible. If the movement is unpopular and behaves rapaciously towards the population, there will be few volunteers. Able young men who feel they can survive outside the protection of the village will escape from an approaching 'battalion'. Children, captured civilians and surrendered enemies are usually an important source of recruits in these circumstances. In all cases, loyalty is a problem and Lumpen leaders will make an effort to indoctrinate recruits. Children may be forced to commit atrocities against their own families, and will be renamed in order to render them outcasts from their communities.[39] Child soldiers are mainly used for administrative purposes, as runners, servants, porters and for reconnaissance. Although they can be made obedient and resolute in the face of danger, they are too slight for effective combat with small arms. The tragedy of this process is that the child soldiers can become inured to bush living with an armed group, and may even return to a 'battalion' from resettlement shelters.

Former warriors give vague and inconsistent accounts of their training for combat. Most agree that the training process takes about two to three weeks, and includes fitness and drill. In Liberia, witnesses observed an emphasis on indoctrination.[40] Some rounds are fired so that recruits can practise holding and aiming their weapons. Most warriors can strip and clean their weapons with great facility. However, the training period is far too short and informally conceived to achieve military reliability.

Lumpen forces appear to fight mostly for resources and supplies. The fighting is ritualised, and a fighter will be unlucky to be hit by an aimed shot from an opposing warrior. The sound of gunfire is almost as important as the impact of the shot. A successful attack empowers the group, replenishing its stocks of ammunition, food and recruits, as well as enriching its warriors with loot. A failed attack greatly diminishes a unit's fighting capability, and will reduce it to banditry with empty weapons and machetes until it can get more ammunition. Lumpen forces tend to melt way under bombardment by indirect fire weapons.

In the scale of insurgent types, Lumpen forces tend to be the weakest. They emerge and thrive where there is a vacuum of power, particularly in a collapsing state. The Lumpen's *ad hoc* power structures are fragile, leading to fighting and rivalry between battalions and between personalities within a battalion. In a weak state where the monopolies of power and the use of force have eroded, the Lumpen force is dangerous and usually careless of humanitarian codes. But faced with experienced troops from a more professional army, the Lumpen fighter has a poor record and the resolve of units to stay and fight evaporates. Lumpens use violence more to secure their day-to-day living than to prosecute a long-term political strategy. Their fighting techniques have a ritualistic character, and their intent is to drive off rather than confront the adversary. The survivability of a Lumpen unit is reduced by its lack of popular support and its relatively undeveloped international framework.

The clan insurgent force

Clan is from the Gaelic word *clann*, meaning children, the descendants of a common ancestor. In Scotland, the word described the

Highland communities that were divided by topography and distinctive surnames. A Scottish clan was a legal and practical community, a biological corporation in which children were taught to name the chief, the chief's genealogy and their own. From the Somali coast eastwards to Kashmir, society is also organised by clans, with distinctions of language, ethnicity and name. The clan, with its loyalties of blood, kinship and tradition, is a powerful unifying force that can be mobilised for military purposes. The Scottish clans became the Highland Regiments of the British Army and, in the Northwest Frontier Provinces, the Afridi, the Utman Khel, the Mohmands and distant tribes from within Afghanistan enlisted to the Pathans, Khyber Rifles and the Frontier Force Regiments of Pakistan. The potential for clans or tribes to be organised as a military force distinguishes them from less-structured ethnic groups. Although the Northern Irish Catholic community, the Basques and the Tamils in Sri Lanka also provide a cultural source of energy for insurgency, their social structures are less significant to the organisation of their clandestine forces.

Superficially, the operating methods and general conduct of a clan force have similarities to the Lumpen insurgency. Furthermore, urban areas of Somalia, Pakistan and Afghanistan are a refuge for an increasing number of Lumpen-type youths who also provide an element of the rank and file of a clan insurgent force. Despite these similarities, there are important differences which justify 'the clan' as a separate category. The major source of a clan's power is derived from its social structure in a way that it is not in a Lumpen force. At the lowest level, the loyalties of clan fighters to their immediate group are dictated by their genealogy, which is transparent and cannot be changed.[41] Lumpen warriors do not fight in a family group, and individual loyalty is less stable; they may change sides in any direction during a campaign. A clan's fighting unit is organised from a traditional structure, which gives its leader authority. A Lumpen structure is artificial, and may collapse from within or fall apart under pressure; when it does, the rank and file are free to return to the population as individuals. A clan cannot be demobilised in the same way, and its dispersal or social reorientation cannot be regarded as a development goal for rehabilitation. At the end of a campaign, the structures which have empowered an insurgent force may be weakened, but they can be resuscitated. Clans and tribes alter slowly: the Somali clan system, for instance, is largely unchanged by the three international interventions of the last decade; Afghanistan's ability to enclose and then expel its invaders is also a demonstration of clan survivability.

Survival motivation

To survive at all, the clan member needs to be physically fit, self-reliant, resourceful and wilfully independent. The tension between the individuality of rural tribespeople and their need to submit themselves to a collective system for survival has, in Somalia, been characterised as a pastoral democracy. In it, individual views are valued, but after deliberation a collective decision is taken. The deliberative approach to problems is manifested at every level of a clan organisation. Judgements on which course of action to take or whose suit to prefer are made by elders. At every level, an elder represents the family, the extended family and the sub-clan, and their influence is derived from the support of their particular group.

Individuals do not support the clan for sentimental reasons, but because it is the key to their survival. In a very harsh rural environment, there are few alternative occupations from which to sustain a living. Seifulaziz Milas explains it thus: 'The values of Somali society are those of survival, of survivors in a pastoral nomadic society struggling for life in a harsh desert setting where the cost of a mistake is often death.'[42]

Somalis live in isolated kin-groups, which have to compete for limited resources, water and land.[43] They cannot survive beyond the support of the clan and its components. Each member has to recognise that survival depends on putting the needs of the group before those of the individual. In return, the clansman is vested with security. If members of the family are harmed, 'their kinship groups are obliged to seek revenge or payment of blood compensation from the kinship group of the killer. If they kill, their kinship group must protect them from revenge or help them to pay blood compensation to the kinship group or clan of the victim'.[44] Life outside the protection of the clan is therefore at best extremely risky. The vital resources which are protected by the clan are no longer available to the excommunicated. They become a prey to all, their security and status have been removed, they are outlawed and no one will avenge the robberies and rape visited on them. This collective support extends into every area of competition, including employment, business deals and political opportunities.[45]

The distinction between the individual motivation in a clan and in a Lumpen force is that, in the latter, the individual joins from the outside, whereas clan people are born within it. They had no options, and will have to support the system if all its members are to survive. This is a uniquely strong reason for them to remain loyal.

A family cannot isolate itself; it is fixed on a 'genealogical grid' that determines its relationship to all the branches of its clan, and to other clans.[46] According to Milas, Somali children are taught, in the same way as clan children were in the Scottish Highlands, to 'memorise the names of their ancestors. By reciting their personal lines of decent, two total strangers can quickly position themselves in the Somali grid ... During the civil war in Somalia, this convergence on occasion became a matter of life or death'.[47]

Deliberative processes are also used to regulate violence between clans and diminish the impact of disasters. An impending confrontation can be forestalled in a civil manner and a deal can emerge, which prevents further collective bloodshed, although the individual culprit may have to pay the price of a reckless act. The clan also protects its members in times of extreme adversity. In Somalia during the famines and violence of the 1990s, the clan safety net did not operate uniformly, but thousands who fled Mogadishu and other war-torn areas were sheltered by their clans in their areas of origin. This protective obligation also operates in the growing Afghan and Somali diaspora.

The environment
A clan is tempered by the rules governing its survival, the presence of competing clans, the pressures of violence around them and the efforts of foreign powers to alter the local situation. These conditions comprise an environment rather than an opposing force. Global change has not altered the clans' continued reliance on

scarce commodities such as water, grazing and arable land. Never-theless, the growing wealth and importance of urban areas exercise an attraction which increasingly compels family groups to decide between their rural manifestation and the prospect of participating in, and exploiting, a wealthier urban society. While a clan remains based in its rural environs, the rigours of survival continue to impose strict codes of collective discipline. Both the group and the individual have to be strong to survive. In addition to the harsh-ness of their physical environment, the presence of other clans competing for the same resources discourages their degeneration. Strength, cohesion and collective discipline are attributes that can be readily translated into a military force. In the case of the clan, they are not so much the consequence of a formidable opposing force, as of the environment itself.

A clan is also conditioned by living in a war zone. Warfare does not confront the clan with an unaccustomed shock of life and death contingencies: a clan lives continuously with such emerg-encies. Nevertheless, living in a constant war zone brings other conditions: a saturation of small arms, an environment polluted with abandoned munitions and unexploded ordnance and, in the case of Afghanistan, the constant danger of anti-personnel mines.

The manifestation of the warring clan also implies an absence of government. In Somalia and Afghanistan, national regimes, invaders and civil wars come and go, but the clan structures seem to survive. However, in the 1990s civil war and the intensified competition for political power and resources corrupted the clan system. The venality of the warlords and their disregard for humanitarian principles eroded the clan, diminished the significance of the elders and encouraged a new generation of *mooryaan*, former street children who have grown up outside the clan in dangerous urban areas. The implication of these develop-ments on the structure of the clan insurgent force is explained in the next section.

Organisation of a clan's armed force

Although a clan's social structures have survived generations of civil war and invasion, they are nevertheless under pressure.

Global changes have energised urban areas, and new ways of making money require a more interdependent approach that cuts across traditional structures. As a result, the organisation of the clan is no longer static; byzantine social compromises are afoot that hope to protect the traditional element of the clan, and at the same time exploit urban areas. The process is continuous and also highly relevant to the clan's capability to deploy armed forces. This section describes the more traditional system of organising an armed force from a rural clan, and explains the problems in adapting this structure to the urban environment.

A clan armed force is a manifestation of its own culture, and imports very little of the nomenclature of international staff systems or insurgent doctrines. Its structures are minimal and its rank systems informal. Nevertheless, the individual who is appointed to control carries the authority of the clan in a way that a Lumpen lieutenant does not. In the social structure (as opposed to the armed force that is derived from it), the highest appointment may be a single chief or a group of chiefs representing each part of the clan. Below him or them, there is a council of elders appointed by the sub-clans. Below them, each family or sub-sub-clan will also have a system of elders. When a clan mobilises its manpower into an armed faction, it will appoint a war leader. He is selected on much the same basis as a managing director or a chief executive officer (CEO), and needs to be able to show that he has a record of successful combat. A war leader in a clan system therefore does not raise and motivate his own insurgent force from a few armed followers, as Taylor and Sankoh did, but is appointed to manage an existing body. Consequently, his relationship to the elders and chiefs is similar to that of a CEO's to a board of directors and shareholders. War leaders who are unsuccessful or offend the clan ethos by their behaviour can be suspended. The power of the clan elders is maintained by their control of recruits and funds. However, this relationship is changing, and for over a decade war leaders have reduced their dependency on the clan by generating their own separate sources of recruits and wealth. Nevertheless, for all the reasons described in the previous section, the imperatives of survival and kinship continue to weigh in favour of the authority of the clan elders.

Within the clan, each family sends young men to serve in an armed faction either because the clan is threatened and has collectively decided to move on to a war footing, or in times of comparative peace individuals may have an urge for adventure. In both Somalia and Afghanistan, civil war and humanitarian emergencies have considerably interrupted education and, as a result, many recruits are barely literate. They will nevertheless have an extensive oral account of their genealogy. The recruit takes with him a clan weapon and presents himself to the war leader, or more likely to his particular family group within the faction. Some recruits may be as young as 11 years old. Weapons are usually the property of the immediate family of the recruit, and are on the whole 1970s and 1980s versions of the AK47, AR15 and G3.

A clan's sources of income vary according to its territorial possessions and international interests. In the absence of a government, clans divide the resources of the state and its revenue-raising opportunities between themselves in much the same way as they divide up the life-sustaining resources of the desert. The most common method is to extort money from individuals or groups with goods passing across their territory. In return for payment, travellers receive a safe conduct which runs out at the next inter-tribal or clan boundary. This system flourishes in most tribal and clan areas from the Caucasus to the Hindu Kush and beyond. In Somalia, the absence of government has allowed considerably greater opportunity for revenue collection, which includes: providing foreign companies with opportunities for dumping dangerous waste, the illegal allocation of Somalia's offshore fisheries to foreign fleets and the transaction of pirated cargoes. Clans will also levy tolls at key bridges, mountain passes, airports and coastal ports. At the edge of an urban area, a clan will tax vehicles, farm produce, the supply of water, fuel and charcoal, and activities in market areas. On a smaller scale, each family unit is also a business, with income from its agricultural surplus if there is one, minor extortion and interest from property. An important element of the clan's funds may also come from abroad, in particular from Arab states, which support the clan for domestic or foreign-policy reasons, as well as from Somali and Afghan communities living overseas. Although a sizeable number are refugees and therefore extremely poor, there is also a significant amount of financial traffic between the overseas element and the clan itself. Institutionally, the clan can use these overseas funds for the purchase of special equipment, including medical supplies and weapons.

When the clan leader is in a dependent relationship to the council of elders, he receives funds through the clan. The war leader's authority is therefore derived from the clan. In a pastoral democracy, individual fighters will challenge him, but absolute disaffection carries the huge penalty of being excommunicated. In a traditional faction, this is usually an unbearable punishment.

The clan-dependent fighting force can be eroded for several reasons. In periods of comparative peace the threat to the clan diminishes, and the 'board of directors' scale down their financial and manpower support. Global changes have also raised the prospect of a war leader becoming independent of the clan, and making considerable sums of money for himself in the manner of a Lumpen insurgent leader. These pressures are most visible at the lowest level. Even under ideal conditions, a clan fighting force is made up from several different families, which sub-divide into smaller groups, each representing a different family interest.

Clans in urban areas

The classic model described above is under threat. Randolph Kent, Director of the UN Development Programme in Somalia, maintains that the Somalis' struggle for survival now has less to do with the strains of nomadic existence and more to do with an economy that is dramatically affected by a lack of capital investment, under-development, the absence of infrastructure and sporadic violence.[48] Values are undermined by the increasing use of locally-available drugs and family discipline and structures become weakened, nowhere more dangerously than in a clan's fighting elements.[49] When populations move into the city, the traditionally-organised clan tends to erode as it comes into contact with the financial systems that operate in urban areas.[50] In the collision of cultures, global and financial forces appear to be stronger than the nomad survival ethic. Although urban areas under clan or tribal control may not have the appearance of modernity, the extended reach of global communications ensures that, behind the ancient façades, extremely modern approaches to grey-area trading and capital transfer are in operation. The clan's apparent cohesion becomes increasingly under stress by this environment. Several different clan communities hold the urban areas. In contrast to the demographic separations imposed by desert and mountain, family groups from different clans live together in the same confined space. The urban area is too complicated to be regulated by the absolute system of a clan; whereas resources in the wilderness are divided between families and clans, in an urban system they are shared. At the lowest level, small traders cannot survive if they rely entirely on a particular clan for their raw materials, sources of fuel and electricity, financial transfers, protection and custom. Even in Mogadishu, the systems which sustain the city have to connect with each other despite being run by different clans and sub-clans. Consequently, a new class of businessmen has emerged that survives, not in their clan affiliation, but within less formal and less exclusive structures such as the Shari'a courts. When the traditional armed faction encounters the urban system, it begins to erode from the bottom up. Family groups begin to work individually with businessmen, mainly offering protection for their property and the safe transit of goods and money. The family group may also indulge in its own business activities, as well as some light extortion.

Clan war leaders also help in the disintegration of their own fighting forces by striking deals with businesses on an individual basis or for their immediate family group, as opposed to the entire clan. When this happens, the clan's appointed war leader grows more distanced from the clan elders. The distancing is mutual. The elders tend to reduce the scale of their support for the war leader, who thus enjoys less of the elders' authority in the eyes of his fighters. As a result, he has to adopt the controlling techniques of the Lumpen lieutenant, including drugs and violent punishment.

In Somalia, social structures in the city are additionally confused by the presence of the *mooryaan*. According to Roland Marchal, *mooryaan* is a derogatory term meaning parasite, the very poor, the rural bums, who in the Habargidir areas sleep next to the cattle pens at night for warmth and protection.[51] In Mogadishu, they live in abandoned or liberated apartments in mixed groups, comprising youths from different clans held together by personal linkages, as they would be in a non-traditional urban society. In the eyes of the conservative Somali, the *mooryaan* are associated with extremes of savagery and brutal behaviour, with the inventive use of drugs, unorthodox sexual practices and rape. There are several different manifestations of *mooryan*. The most dissolute and dangerous are described by Marchal as the 'new generation' groups.[52] These tend to live outside the clan and family structures; they will stay at a particular venue for a short time, during which they may collectively rob a particular target before breaking up and re-forming into different configurations at new venues. Another type of *mooryaan* tends to coalesce around a 'technical', normally a pick-up truck with a medium-calibre machine gun mounted on it. The technical *mooryan* are likely to remain together around the nucleus of an armed vehicle for longer, and will use it as a business asset, for hire and protection. A more politically-motivated *mooryaan* group has a tradition of rioting to demonstrate 'the intensity of a demand or a dissatisfaction and always [find] an overstocked shop or overly furnished office ... to launch them into a debate on the redistribution of wealth'.[53]

The tension between the emerging metropolitan society and the clan system is unresolved. Even the *mooryaan*, who appear to have forsaken every vestige of a tribal lifestyle, will deal cautiously with an envoy from their own kin. The linkage between the *mooryaan* and the clan elders survives, and greatly complicates hostage negotiations with a group of urban captors who may represent several clans. On a much larger scale, in the face of an outside threat detached communities in the city will remuster to the clan. In particular, the threatening presence of a foreign force has in the past acted to assemble a dispersed clan. In these circumstances, the family groups which have become separated from the war leader's faction will return, bringing with them a sizeable element of the *mooryaan*. The active strength of a clan fighting force is therefore hard to calculate. The figures are altered by day-to-day tensions in rural areas, as well as by competing interests in the city.

Operating methods

Although a clan force is distinct from a Lumpen force in its sources of support and social structure, its approach to combat is similar. Like the Lumpen force, clans and tribes fight mainly for resources. In the past, they fought over essential issues vital to their survival, such as grazing land, water and freedom of movement. Today, their motivation for fighting has a greater sense of self-enrichment. The defined objectives of the past have become complicated by multiparty interests, as in the case of import monopolies, drug markets and the exercise of financial control. Ostensibly, clans and tribes fight under the banners of a political party. However, in the case of the Somali, a fighting group may be affiliated to several parties, and despite the visibility of politicians and their appearance as agenda-setters, some observers maintain that party acronyms are foreign to clan culture. Party titles provide respectability in the eyes of overseas donors, attract foreign aid and are local symbols of an existing alliance, but they are seldom the real reason for a clan to fight and kill. In the clan ethos, there is also a strong looting culture, and historically there was confusion between public and private property. According to Marchal, in Somalia the looting culture was exacerbated by Siad Barre's regime, which advocated war as a way of seizing property. These behavioural aberrations are not challenged by the new metropolitan social structures.[54]

Because clans and tribes tend to flourish in areas where there is an absence of governance, the military proficiency of opposing forces is usually low. The short interventions of international forces in Mogadishu and Kabul have not been long enough or sufficiently imposing to alter the proficiency of local clans and tribes. In Afghanistan, tribesmen had a formidable reputation as long-range marksmen, as well as mastery in the use of ground and low-level tactics.[55] But in the post-Cold War era, clan fighters' marksmanship is generally poor and individual fieldcraft reckless. The clan will fight fiercely and effectively when an installation that is vital to their survival is contested or, as in the case of Mogadishu in 1993, when a foreign force challenges their territorial integrity. However, in day-to-day confrontations violence is ritualised, as it is in the Lumpen fighting culture. An incident between two armed family groups will begin with abusive shouting, tensions escalate with weapons' pointing, parties then fire into the air or on to the ground close to the adversaries' feet, and finally the groups will shoot to kill. This ritual is not followed in the case of an ambush or a revenge attack, where the faction has previously decided to carry out a set-piece surprise attack. Sometimes, in the case of gradually rising tension and competition between two groups, actual violence can be forestalled by the intervention and negotiation of clan elders. There are many procedures 'worked out by fighters to make it possible for them to defer a real armed conflict, while at the same time claiming their rights over some goods or stressing the necessity of respecting agreements made at the level of sub-clans, of the clans, even (more rarely) of the political leaders'.[56]

Although clans possess indirect support weapons, there is little effort to use them to their full effect. Mortars are fired without the use of sights or gridded maps. A mortar attack can take place over several days, and corrections are made by visual adjustment or, in urban areas, by sending in reconnaissance groups posing as road-sweepers to check the fall of shot. There appear to be no formal arrangements for training new arrivals to the fighting group. In 1993 in urban areas of Mogadishu, groups of snipers were effective, but this does not elevate the generally poor standard of marksmanship. In a clan or a tribe, the fighter's weapon is carried as a fashion accessory which, according to its model, denotes the importance of the owner. They may be swiftly brought into action at close quarters, but the semi-automatic rifle is a stand-off weapon, and few clan fighters are sufficiently well-trained to use it for that purpose.[57] In Somalia, fighters over the age of 30 may have been trained during service in the Somali Armed Forces. They will pass on their knowledge, especially in the use of support weapons and technicals.

For the purposes of estimating their significance as actors in a wider peace-force intervention or a conflict zone, the fighting units organised from clans are distinct from the Lumpen forces described earlier. In the scale of insurgent forces, a clan force is more formidable than a Lumpen. Clan forces have prevailed against the more powerful armies of richer states, significantly the Soviets in Afghanistan in the 1980s and US forces in Mogadishu in

1993. The structure of the clan is stronger and more durable than that of the Lumpen force. It has been tested over several hundred years as an extended organisation, designed to ensure the survival of its members. Nevertheless, a clan is not socially isolated or moribund, but has to react to its environment. As the pace of urbanisation accelerates, the clan will be altered, and the distinctions between its fighting elements and the more modern Lumpen forces will begin to blur. Although urban growth diminishes the clan force as a survival need, this does not guarantee that the insurgent culture that replaces it will necessarily be less formidable, or easier to deal with.

Popular insurgent forces

The concept of insurgency, whereby a small group sets out to overthrow a larger and more powerful regime, relied in its original form on the empowering nature of popular assistance. 'Popular' therefore refers to the support of a population, which expands with great energy and overwhelms the more powerful forces of the opposing government. In the classic form, a popular insurgent leader starts with just a few followers, and prepares the political environment for the campaign (the 'Pre-Revolutionary Phase'). As it gains more supporters, the movement becomes active and begins its operations against government forces (the 'Insurgency Phase'). If this is successful and the insurgent forces are sufficiently powerful, insurgency turns to civil war (the 'Limited War Phase').[58] A popular insurgency reaches its culmination when the incumbent regime collapses, as it did in Saigon in 1975, or when a third party intervenes to organise a transfer of power, as the Commonwealth Monitoring Force (CMF) did in Zimbabwe-Rhodesia in 1980, and the UN in Namibia in 1989.

Although global change has made it possible to challenge governments using resource exploitation as a source of support, popular insurgents still exist and operate successfully. The principles of popular insurgency are generic and are manifested in some form in most insurgent movements. Nevertheless, the concept is not static, and has evolved under the pressures of global change. In the 1990s, popular insurgents developed their own sources of wealth. An element of the LTTE became an international corporation to provide an operating income; UNITA, which was already in a resource-rich conflict area, reorganised itself to exploit Angola's raw materials. Increased migration and international labour also play a significant part in overseas funding activities.

Whereas Lumpen and clan forces operate successfully in a weak state, in a richer and stronger state with a better-educated population and stronger security forces, only a robust popular movement can survive. Popular insurgent forces are a response to a stronger state in which the insurgent has less freedom of movement, and needs to be better organised. Young people who become activists in a popular insurgency have greater freedom of choice, and are more self-motivated and less brutally disciplined than their Lumpen peers. Popular insurgencies are more vigorously opposed and have to organise themselves secretively, with complex structures that are less easy to penetrate. Their campaigns can last for several decades, and tend to be stalemated, wearing down the population, eroding democratic institutions and brutalising the participants.

Environment and opposition forces

In the early years of the Cold War, the Maoist versions of popular insurgency took place in mountains, deserts and tropical rainforests, where retreating Western powers were pressured to abandon their colonial possessions by nationalist forces. Global change shrank the wilderness areas and moved populations towards townships and crowded suburbs. By the 1980s, while some popular insurgencies survived in the wilderness, a new strain began to flourish in high-density urban environments.

In Greece, Spain, Northern Ireland, Israel and Sri Lanka, there are no genuine wilderness areas. Governments have been democratically elected and the state itself is wealthier. Compared to states where Lumpen and clan forces flourish, wealth is more widely distributed, the government raises revenue from taxes, the population is better educated, literacy rates are higher and there are more survival alternatives for young school-leavers. The counter-insurgent strategy is conducted visibly, the media is more developed, more households possess radios and televisions and more newspapers are read. Constant visibility influences the insurgents' campaign; incidents are staged to achieve the widest publicity and to effect maximum discredit on the government. Reporters are called in advance to witness a damaging riot; a car bomb is exploded late in the afternoon so as to become tomorrow's headlines. Front-page editors amplify the effect of a small explosion and a few casualties to reverberate dramatically and continuously around the entire population.

The opposing security forces are very much more effective and dangerous to the insurgent. Institutional memory is better and civil servants understand how to educate politicians and the public to maintain their political conviction in the face of casualties. Field commanders are more experienced and do not indulge in the reactive acts of oppression that the insurgents are hoping to incite. Government intelligence forces have had many years to recruit informants, infiltrate the movement and develop technical surveillance that intrudes into every detail of the insurgency. These threats require the popular insurgent force to be more skilfully organised and to operate in a measured and determined manner. The insurgent's relationship to its opposition is defined by an equation: a tough regime invites a dangerous insurgent.

Motivation

Most states are divided by culture, ethnicity and opportunity, and by poverty and wealth. Popular insurgent energy springs from a particular segment of the population, which feels unbearably excluded by one or more of these divisions.[59] Today's popular insurgent forces attract young, energetic recruits for the same reasons as 60 years ago, when they challenged colonial powers.

Philosophically, it is unjustifiable for a minority to seek to overthrow a democratic system solely because of feelings of exclusion. A minority has recourse to persuade a government to recognise them, and may bring pressure to bear by civil disobedience. But when the majority imposes a condition on a minority that becomes a source of outrage, the minority's arrogant sense of their own rightness licences their violence and philosophical problems disappear. The increasingly violent minority sees itself as morally right and therefore justified in acting beyond the law, especially when there seems to be no peaceful avenue along which to present their case.[60] In the case of the LTTE, the Tamil minority saw themselves being excluded by an elected Sinhalese government that proscribed their language, prospects of education, professional employment and ethnicity.[61] In this context, the LTTE provided an attractive combination of success, bravado and Tamil nationalism, which acted as a restorative for Tamil self-respect.[62] Although the LTTE grew from the impetus of its operations, it also developed a manifesto and a constitution. These articulated the need for self-determination and a homeland (a Tamil *eelam*) where Tamils could have the autonomy to organise their own security, prosperity and governance. These were rousing issues for an excluded Tamil population.[63]

In Liberia and Sierra Leone, the young men and women who initially joined insurgent forces also felt excluded from society. Their motives, and the techniques used to mobilise their rebellious spirit, were in principle the same as those of a popular force. The difference lies in the manifestation of the Lumpen and the popular movements; beyond the revolutionary rhetoric, which is often similar, it is what they do in the field that distinguishes them. Popular insurgents need the political and physical support of the population. Their organisation reflects this, and they operate in a way that husbands the support of the local community.

Organisation

A popular insurgent force is organised along carefully considered, functional lines, which tend to be elaborate and cellular. Individuals and organisations, whose real identity as part of the movement is concealed, may function openly, for example as school teachers or trade unions.[64] Some elements are required to raise funds and manage income and overseas interests. Most modern popular insurgent forces will need to deal effectively in several different functional areas at once. The broad categories of their activity are: finances and fund-raising; international linkages; politics and the media; and military operations. Whereas all insurgencies may deal informally from time to time in these areas, the popular insurgent's organisation is distinct in that each function is defined, and appointees are carefully chosen, vested with authority and expected to function for some time.

A popular movement's organisation reveals its real intent more accurately than the rhetoric of a manifesto. There is a strong relationship between its structure and the appeal it makes to the supporting population. If a popular insurgency is proclaiming self-determination, then it should reflect structures designed for that purpose, and not be overwhelmingly organised for grey-area trading and the exploitation of natural resources. A popular force should also reserve some of its campaign energy for husbanding and encouraging public support. These aspects are particularly well-organised in the case of *Hamas* and *Hizbollah*, which have elaborate structures of subordinated NGOs for health, education, women's recognition, relief and religion.[65]

Popular movements receive an increasing proportion of their funds from overseas. The LTTE's international arrangements are well-developed and organised in the manner of an international corporation, of which Prabhakaran is the managing director. Its financial offices, which are ostensibly legitimate, are organised by the LTTE's chief finance officer, K. P. Kummaruppa; they are located in Thailand, with branches in the UK and Australia. Its investment income is unknown. Some of its capital is deployed as shipping (see Table 1), and LTTE ships are legally registered and insured. According to Sri Lankan intelligence sources, they may, however, be diverted from a routine journey to deliver cargo to the Jaffna area.[66] Tamil diaspora businesses in Canada, the UK, Australia, Malaysia and the Nordic states provide income. LTTE weapon imports have been mainly from South Africa, Myanmar, Thailand, Afghanistan and Ukraine (mainly for plastic explosives).

An increasing number of Tamils are being convicted as drug couriers, and Sri Lankan intelligence sources estimate that 75% of Tamils carrying drugs may be part of LTTE drug operations. However, evidence is circumstantial and a definite link cannot be made. The LTTE's local sources of income include farming, tea estates, bus companies, printing, photographic studios and several small factories making soap, syrup, jam, soft drinks and joss-sticks.[67] Other income is derived from the taxation of cigarettes and imported goods in LTTE-held areas. The LTTE regularly robbed

Table 1 LTTE merchant ships ('Sea Pigeons')†

IMO no.	Name	Tonnage (gross)	Port/flag	Name	Fate
				LTTE merchant ship losses	
6424014	**Venus**	2,796	**Batumi/Georgia**	**Cholakeri**	Capsized off Thai coast, 28/11/92
	Previous LTTE names: Laluna del Mar I, MGO 1, Ola, Victory 9, Victory, Omiros, Sun Bird, Iliyana			**Yahata** (sometimes named Ahat)	Scuttled by crew after being intercepted by the Indian Navy off Jaffna, Sri Lanka, 16/1/93
6602018	**Baris B**	999	**Valletta/Malta**		
	Previous LTTE names: Swene, Mariya, Golden Bird, Saint Anthonys, Sofia				

Continued . . . .

Table 1 Continued

6618524	Viking Carrier	755	St Lorenzo/Honduras	Horizon (Previously named Julex-Comex 3, Commes-Joux and Comex-Joux 3)	Destroyed by Sri Lankan forces off Trincomalee, Sri Lanka, 14/2/96
	Previous LTTE names: Penaga, Sea Pearl I, Cholan				
3500506	Emerald	1,150	St Lorenzo/Honduras	Stillus Limmasul (sometimes named Limmasul)	Destroyed by the Sri Lankan Air Force off Mullaitivu, Sri Lanka, 2/11/97
	Previous LTTE names: Pethiya, Yelicia				
3517664	Progress	1,351	Phnom-Penh/Cambodia		
	Previous LTTE names: Olivia, Sea Horse				

Source: Compiled by James Foster from interviews and from Lloyds Shipping Intelligence.

†Other LTTE ships for which there are no official records are reported to have used the names **Ichulite, Ali Joshing, Amazon and Tongnova**

banks, which provided a significant source of income during the last decade.[68]

Insurgent forces tend to establish a political office separate from their operational wing. The political element may be an overt and lawful political party, which represents the insurgent manifesto in a peaceful manner. The relationship to the operations wing varies in each movement. In most cases, the operational wing's activities, especially acts of terrorism against a civil population, are difficult to reconcile with the public face of the movement as represented by the political office. Sinn Fein, the political wing of the IRA, has difficulty in reconciling bombings and civilian casualties with its vote-seeking efforts. In Israel/Palestine, actions by maverick cells strain the relationship between *Hamas* and the Palestine Liberation Organisation (PLO).[69] In the LTTE, Prabhakaran's dominating leadership reaches into each division of his organisation and achieves a greater unity of effort. The LTTE's 'popularity' in its own areas is to some extent induced by fear as well as a genuine admiration for its activities. During the LTTE's occupation of Jaffna, its puritanical standards and ruthlessness acted against it, and local Tamils were relieved when it was forced to abandon the town. By 2000, Prabhakaran had responded by instituting a group of personal envoys whose job it is to travel among the Tamil population, listen to grievances against the LTTE and impart Prabhakaran's latest thoughts on Tamil *eelam*.[70] The tactical wing is also careful to recognise the sacrifice of casualties by visiting families and publishing obituary notices.

Popular insurgents use public relations as a weapon. The LTTE rarely extorted from Tamils and would compensate locals for the seizure of vehicles or use of buildings.[71] In Sinhala areas, the same LTTE speaks cold-bloodedly of hijacking vehicles, killing occupants and massacring families in their homes.[72] *Hizbollah* uses television aggressively, and has recorded 75% of its operations for transmission on Hebrew satellite services.[73] Foreign visitors are treated particularly carefully by political wings. In UNITA's Jamba enclave, visitors encountered Chinese-style political posters with messages for domestic and overseas audiences and crowds of apparently happy locals, while free contact with genuine families was strictly limited.[74]

Table 2 Outline of some tactical organisations in the LTTE

Selected independent units	Black Tigers	Special forces elite Suicide cadres
	Sea Tigers	Maritime operations
Staff functions	Communications	Satellite communications High frequency between bases VHF patrol level Commercial VHF
	Support weapons	Anti-aircraft unit Medium mortar unit
	Logistics	Transport Food Clothing
	Survey	GPS Map stocks Map-making
	Intelligence	Prabhakaran's Central Intelligence Tactical intelligence
	Explosives	Mines storage and manufacture Bombs and suicide devices

Source: Compiled by James Foster from interviews with Sri Lankan Security Force Staff.

The tactical organisation is functional, and reflects the technical skills of the group's more educated rank and file. Table 2 shows the degree of military sophistication in the LTTE.

A distinguishing feature of a popular insurgency is the controlling method used within fighting units. LTTE fighters are motivated by their own commitment and self-respect; junior commanders are appointed by the institution, and there is therefore less need for them to behave in a frightening and brutal manner towards their followers. Young Tamils seldom choose to join the

LTTE as a last resort for survival, but leave school in order to do so. They come from a highly literate society, and are likely to have completed an element of their secondary education. When they join they are treated with the same respect as a recruit in a regular military force. The training regime is arduous and instructors may slap or cuff a recruit, but more usually as an act of admonishment and not by using a stick. Training also includes a considerable amount of education, in which the tenets of Tamil *eelam* are emphasised. Fighters' self-development is encouraged by streaming them according to their skills. Those with special aptitude will become bomb- and mine-makers, global positioning system (GPS) operators, radio technicians, armourers or mechanics; artists are even taught to draw maps. If they were not fully committed before joining, their sense of obligation is strengthened after they sign the constitution which requires them to put the cause before family and lovers, and to expect death if they quit or form splinter groups.[75] Each fighter receives a cyanide capsule, which is usually hung like a badge of office around the neck; women fighters carry two.[76] These procedures ensure a degree of political commitment and self-respect that distinguishes the popular insurgency from the Lumpen and clan force.

The cadre of suicide bombers is separated from the rest. Most are selected from a background of intense personal trauma involving the rape, murder and destruction of immediate family. The mantra of indoctrination reminds them of these facts, and is intended to spur them to their final act of revenge. Within the LTTE, suicide bombers keep together as a privileged group. In Palestinian insurgent organisations, suicide bombers may commit themselves nominally, and then live normally with their families for some time before their final indoctrination session, after which they become living martyrs for a short period prior to their final operation.

As a rule, leaders of popular insurgencies are ruthless men, who successfully combine charm and the determined destruction of their rivals. Prabhakaran is notoriously resolute in his elimination of LTTE leaders who might challenge or embarrass him, or stray from the path of Tamil *eelam*. His information comes to him from his personal group of Central Intelligence officers, whose job is to monitor the movement. They are carefully selected for their loyalty and lack of ambition. A challenging personality who is destined for assassination is first publicly criticised and discredited. Prabhakaran's disciplinary reach extends to France and Canada, where he has arranged the murder of renegade LTTE figures. He is also able to put pressure on his overseas diaspora through family members remaining in Sri Lanka. Jonas Savimbi used the same controlling methods in UNITA, ensuring that families of commanders and fighters remained at the Jamba enclave while the men were in the field.

Operating methods

The popular insurgents' operating methods vary according to the phase that their campaign has reached. In European countries, IRA derivatives and the Basque separatist group ETA have not managed to progress beyond the insurgent phase, whereas the LTTE has reached the limited war phase. A popular insurgent tends to choose military objectives carefully because they fulfil the strategic aims of the movement. There is therefore a separation of effort; the purely logistic targets, which may be banks, armouries and depots, must support the campaign objectives which lie on the critical path of the overall strategy. Logistic targets are routinely attacked, but the campaign objectives are deliberately planned as stages towards achieving the end-state. The characteristic of a popular insurgency is that logistic operations do not become activities in their own right enriching individuals within the movement. When logistic operations obscure the stated aim of the movement, the insurgent force loses its popular distinction and becomes a form of warlordism. A campaign objective may be to threaten government officials of a particular ethnicity, to destroy installations that represent an opposed country or community or, in the limited war phase, to establish or extend a no-go area. Anticipated public response and the likely media reaction will influence the choice of objectives and the manner in which they are attacked.

At a local level, inexperienced popular insurgents may bomb and attack impulsively, but their ultimate success relies on a deliberate approach to the use of violence that is strongly related to their long-term strategy. Prabhakaran is a meticulous planner; in the LTTE's insurgent phase, he would keep an objective under surveillance for several weeks and spend hours developing an elaborate plan of attack.[77] European insurgent groups also show a similarly deliberate approach. A sniper attack in Belfast, for instance, would involve several parties in addition to the sniper, to watch the rear, to conceal and remove the weapon after the attack and to spirit away the principal actors as swiftly as possible from the murder scene. In the LTTE's limited war phase, Prabhakaran continues to demonstrate this capability on a larger military scale. Attacks demand a high degree of coordination between sub-units, which work with each other using radios, and employing principles of surprise and concentration of effort familiar to regular armed forces.

The insurgent force will attack or ambush a target, which through reconnaissance and planning it already knows it can overwhelm. The attack is usually pushed to its conclusion with immense determination. Successful popular insurgents have to suppress their instincts for self-preservation to a degree that Lumpen and clan warriors do not. The cyanide capsule symbolises the will to stay and fight. There is nothing ritualistic about the popular insurgents' attack: they shoot with their eyes open, firing aimed shots from the shoulder, they mean to kill their opponents and they cannot abandon their group when the situation turns against them. If their commitment fails there is the fear that their desertion will be punished by death. Prabhakaran's elaborate attacks against the Sri Lankan armed forces are highly sophisticated. Indirect-fire weapons drive the enemy into carefully-prepared minefields. The killing zone has previously been measured out with GPS so that mortars can be registered, or even silent-registered if surprise is important.[78] The action bears all the hallmarks of a professional military operation, and is utterly different from a Lumpen attack in scale, with a different outcome and a different set of reasons for choosing the objective.

The skill of a successful insurgent unit begins with the training and indoctrination of recruits. By 2001, the LTTE's recruits were growing younger; some had scarcely begun their secondary education. After training, boys from 16–18 years tended to go to front-line units, and from 14–16 they remained in the logistic bases.[79] During the early 1990s, an LTTE training camp was described as:

the size of a university campus; a heavily camouflaged jungle town, built in and around a forest clearing. The buildings were surprisingly solid structures of wickerwork, bamboo and thatch: arsenals and hospitals, command huts and dormitories, rest rooms and conference centres, refectories and lecture rooms … with no fewer than 2,000 heavily armed guerrillas attending political lectures, sitting in rapt attention as senior Tigers harangued them with revolutionary rhetoric; others busy with target practice or assault courses or weapon training.[80]

Prabhakaran is personally obsessed with marksmanship, and all recruits pay special attention to being able to shoot accurately. Rambo and Clint Eastwood films are included in the LTTE video library.[81] Videos are frequently used as motivating devices to portray the success of a small group challenging a vastly superior enemy, and LTTE instructors have also used them to illustrate tactical and technical lessons. The LTTE also has a training manual.[82]

The selective use of the LTTE to illustrate the stereotypical popular insurgency implies a unique and classical version which few movements, including the LTTE itself, can live up to. The purpose is to demonstrate in principle how an ideally-motivated and configured popular insurgent force might appear and operate, and how global influences have widened its popular logistic base, but without altering the movement's intensely national agenda.

Popular insurgents can only survive and succeed because they are supported by a sufficient element of the population to sustain them. Their organisation reflects the importance of this relationship. Although Lumpen and clan forces also exhibit the organisational paraphernalia of political wings, these are seldom genuine or effective because in both cases clan and Lumpen fighters are not sustained by popular support. For the popular insurgent, the canvassing, subversion, coercion and organisation of the population are crucial, and have to succeed.

Militarily, the popular insurgent is also distinct from the Lumpen and clan fighter. The popular insurgent is not seeking to drive away opponents, but intends to kill them. To succeed, moves must not be impulsive, but preceded by weeks of calculated planning and reconnaissance. Acts of violence are linked to a political manifesto and logistic targets are a means to an end. When the temptations of personal enrichment overwhelm the political manifesto, the movement ceases to have the distinction of a popular insurgency, the motivating zeal is lost and rubber whips and executions become the instruments of motivation.

The influences of globalisation have enlarged the span of a popular insurgency's objectives to include identity politics. However, this does not alter the essentially national horizon that seems to limit their ambitions. The LTTE may murder Tamil renegades in Paris and London and the IRA has attacked the British overseas, but in both cases these efforts relate to a national agenda.

A global insurgent force

Osama bin Laden and his international network have expanded the definition of insurgency to include a global dimension. Although bin Laden's insurgent energy is a unique phenomenon, his methodology is widely applicable and has attractions for other similarly-dispersed communities. Until global insurgency is completely ruled out as a future option whereby the weak can effectively challenge the strong, the al-Qaeda style of organisation must be regarded as a crucially-important consequence of global change, and possibly even the leading edge of a new chapter of insurgent techniques.

Within the term 'global insurgency', global refers to the movement's sources of energy and support, the environment in which it chooses to fight and the nature of its organisation. A global insurgent force is distinct from Lumpen and clan forces in that the latter tend to be crudely-organised national movements that have a local operating capability. Global insurgents are closer to popular insurgents in organisation, with cellular structures and the constant need to cultivate popular support. They are nevertheless a distinct category, separated from popular forces by the international scope of their intent, their objectives, recruiting base and organisation.[83] The global insurgent faces the most formidable opposition forces of all and, in its efforts to survive, becomes a dangerous and highly-organised manifestation of insurgency, with a demonstrated capability to attack the heart of powerful countries and survive intensive counter-measures.

The motives of the global insurgent

Al-Qaeda and its supporting organisations offer a narrow sample by which to explain the possibility of a trend, a *modus operandi* that can be adopted by similarly-dispersed and deprived populations.[84] Nevertheless, the elements which are significant to future global movements need to be identified. The al-Qaeda phenomenon arises from a widespread feeling of outrage among Muslim populations and migrant communities, combined with the presence of a uniquely-gifted leader, bin Laden, who has been able to mobilise this energy with great success. The social groups that support bin Laden's campaign are from some 60 different countries, and have diverse characteristics.[85] In Islamic states, support comes from displaced and refugee communities, as well as the poor. However, active supporters of al-Qaeda may also be from a wide range of professional classes, including powerful businessmen, teachers, hoteliers, engineers and students. They may be Sunni or Shi'a Muslims; if Shi'a, their support has been coopted through an Iranian initiative in June 1996 to include al-Qaeda's representatives in Hizbollah International. The unique feature of al-Qaeda is that its insurgent energy is derived from an astonishing range of supporters, whose race, culture and professional background vary enormously, but who are nevertheless so concerned for the movement that they will sacrifice their lives. Their common bond is a passionate, in most cases fundamentalist, religious belief. They may also feel a sense of victimisation, and may see the ubiquitous presence of Western democratic, free-market icons as encroaching on Islamic territory, not only in the streets of their cities, but more personally when they travel further afield, imposing Western values on their behaviour, how to conduct business, what to eat, how to dress and even sexual mores. Surrounded by the constant reminders of a palpably successful culture, which so visibly dominates commerce, technology, communications and global security, some Muslim communities may view the world from the perspective of an underclass, whose most intimate sense of identity is also confronted by Western values. The insurgent energy that arises from these circumstances might range from latent animosity to an outrage so powerful as to inspire martyrdom and massacre.

Since the death of Egyptian President Gamal Abdel Nasser in 1967, the Middle East has been starved of charismatic leadership.[86] Until recently, no Arab hero has stepped forward to appease or exploit Muslims' anger and their sense of victimisation. Bin Laden himself felt the heat of this passion during his first spell in Afghanistan in the 1980s. Gradually recognising that Muslim outrage existed on a much wider scale, he harnessed this source of insurgent energy more by reactive instinct than by design. Although his personal details are constantly exposed in the media, several should be emphasised in this context. From the age of seven, bin Laden spent several seasons with Saudi Prince Fahd's children at desert camps organised by his father, Mohammed. This experience gave him first an intuition of the wilderness as well as how to survive there, and second developed invaluable bonds with Saudi Arabia's foremost family. Bin Laden's father was a considerable philanthropist in Jeddah, and the bin Laden family were at the centre of a network of Islamic charities assisting the poor and subsidising pilgrimages to Mecca. When Mohammed died in 1967, 10,000 mourners came to pay their respects. After a dissolute student life in Beirut, bin Laden was converted during a pilgrimage to Mecca in 1977. He set out with several important attributes, including the absolute convictions of a redeemed sinner, a controlling interest in the bin Laden business empire, powerful connections in the Arab world, a genuine organising ability and an instinct for the wilderness.

Bin Laden's motives for deploying these assets for the purposes of insurgency have evolved in an opportunistic manner. This is in contrast to Prabhakaran's steadfast campaign for the LTTE and the Palestinian insurgent movements' long-standing efforts against Israel. Bin Laden's career as an insurgent has several distinct phases: in Afghanistan from 1980, in Sudan from 1991 and again in Afghanistan as the Taliban facilitator from 1996. In each phase, his role has shifted from capacity-builder, bankroller and, finally, as the widely-recognised leader of his own movement. Bin Laden could be regarded as a career insurgent, moving from one manifestation to another in a manner entirely recognisable to a Western business executive. In these different manifestations, it becomes harder to explain precisely what he stands for. His practical operations have been conducted with great precision, but his personal motives have become increasingly vague. In 1989, after winding up a successful campaign against the Soviets in Afghanistan, he returned to Jeddah from the comparative isolation of his base near Peshawar, and was immediately thrust into the floodlights of the Arab media. According to Adam Robinson, 'for one apparently so humble, his determined seduction of the press was extraordinary'.[87] Few requests for interviews were turned down. His business offices created a new department to handle the growing number of inquiries and, during his absence from Jeddah, packets of clippings and videos of his recorded utterances and interviews were despatched to him. Several clues to his real motivation emerge from this period. The interviewers, representing an extraordinary span of interests, found bin Laden to be modest, charming, calm, well-mannered, intelligent and inspirational. Bin Laden thrived on his visibility, signing photos and T-shirts and posing in shops and coffee houses for his voracious admirers. His manifold utterances seemed to adapt themselves to the needs of each interview, and gradually came to cover every dimension of insurrection and life. These included prescriptions for the governments of Saudi Arabia, Egypt, Afghanistan and Lebanon, as well as for the PLO; expelling US forces from Muslim holy places; *jihad*; chemical weapons; life, death and martyrdom; and a united caliphate.[88] His statements had a universal quality that seduced the Arab media and reached a huge Islamic diaspora of potential supporters from different races and cultures. Yet the sum of these ideas did not amount to the manifesto of an insurgent campaign. Bin Laden could tell his audiences with passion what he was against, but less precisely what he was for.

Bin Laden's image as an Arab hero-figure was nevertheless mobilising an audience of millions. His deeds as mujahideen organiser and leader, his declarations on *jihad* and his resistance to Western culture animated young and old, the under-privileged and the excluded from Jakarta to Stockholm. He provided a suitably inspirational manifesto for a disparate mass of Muslims who saw themselves as victims and as an underclass, and his success restored their self-esteem. He had developed a superbly effective rallying cry which cut across a divided Islamic culture, a cry that was comprehensible to every Muslim, strong in condemnation and attractively vague about the future. Bin Laden's multipurpose manifesto was a necessary device to mobilise a very divided constituency of supporters. However, beyond that tactic it is hard to discern a real end-state for his insurgent campaign. He is not a Lumpen warlord, he has lived frugally since his redemption in 1977 and cannot be regarded as a venal man seeking to sustain a rich lifestyle. Does he genuinely desire change? Although he eschews personal luxury, does his self-indulgence take a more sophisticated form? In 1994, during a brief stay in the UK, he was captivated by the mass energy of British football crowds, which he personally witnessed and returned to see several times.[89] Did this experience arouse in him the need for a similarly adoring audience? Are the carefully-styled videos of the modest, white-robed messiah in the wilderness cradling the revolutionary icon, the AK47, more a manifestation of his vanity than the execution of a genuine desire to reach a long-term end-state? Is it more satisfying for him to keep travelling with the aura of a global superstar than to arrive, like Yasser Arafat, in some seedy citadel office? The motivation of al-Qaeda is therefore an uncertain combination; among its followers there is genuine deprivation, a sense of victimisation and a feeling of outrage. Their need for self-respect is met by the messianic bin Laden, the white robed pimpernel figure. But is he driven by anything higher than the need to be all things to all people and a vanity that is not concealed by his disarming modesty?

A global opposition

An insurgent movement that successfully challenges the most powerful states in the world can expect a comprehensive and highly intensive opposition. The global efforts to stamp out al-Qaeda are the antithesis of the depleted forces which customarily stand in the path of the Lumpen insurgent. Bin Laden seemed determined to bring down on himself the most violent retribution. The attacks on USS *Cole* and the US embassies in Nairobi and Dar-es-Salaam had been absorbed without much public attention, but bin Laden continued to challenge America's lack of concern for affairs that lay beyond the country's news vision and conscience.

He succeeded in this aspiration on 11 September 2001, and in doing so unleashed against himself the most powerful counter-strategy in the history of insurgency. The political primacy given to the so-called 'war on terrorism' has raised the US military efforts to destroy al-Qaeda to the level of highest national priority. The US counter-attack has been comprehensive. At the strategic level, political coalitions for military intervention and inter-governmental cooperation have been formed and held together by energetic diplomacy, and in some cases threatening behaviour by the US. Possible refuge states where bin Laden's administrative bases could be re-established have become targets of US political pressure and military menace. At the operational level, the international response was extremely aggressive. The slow-moving coalitions that had deployed so ponderously to the Balkans, East Timor and West Africa in the 1990s were a phenomenon of the past. For bin Laden, the sharp edge of a strategic reaction force arrived immediately in the shape of aircraft carriers, while strategic bombers and surveillance aircraft occupied the skies above. On the ground, the world's most effective fighting units, the Special Air Service (SAS), British and US Marines and US Mountain Division troops spread out into Afghanistan's ravines and mountains to hunt down the 'enemy'. The West was aroused and had mobilised in strength; bin Laden had at last achieved his desire to be taken seriously.

International cooperation extended beyond military force projection to include extradition agreements, the sharing of police, immigration and customs intelligence and concessions for US security agencies to operate inside other nations' borders. Legal procedures were stretched to facilitate the unlawful screening and interrogation of prisoners, and new criminal categories were created to debar the captured mujahideen from prisoner-of-war status or from the civil liberties of a defendant in a Western country. Intrusions into privacy rose sharply. At the highest level, all satellite imagery was re-monopolised by US agencies, and some capability was redeployed to concentrate on potential al-Qaeda targets.[90] Surveillance and screening of the internet and many communication systems, including global shipping movements, private aircraft flights and commercial transactions especially the transfer of cash, intensified. The response has been absolute; the nations of the world are either for or against the US in this affair.

Despite the intensity of the manhunt for bin Laden and his active supporters, he has apparently survived. Prior to his September 2001 strike, he had evidently anticipated the nature of the response and prepared to continue operations in a more dispersed configuration.[91] In this respect, bin Laden is greatly assisted by his environment. Although the US can monitor movement and communications in the most intrusive manner, skilful use of the same technology and a proliferation of communication and information channels also allow the individual to evade detection. Bin Laden's strength is divided between his conventional assets in Afghanistan, which have been considerably damaged by recent operations, and his supporting organisation. The latter is not configured as a military target and survives successfully as an international cellular structure. Each cell is embedded in an open society, where it enjoys the same freedoms of communication, association, movement and commercial opportunity as the host. In this form it is beyond the reach of carrier fleets and regiments of marines. Al-Qaeda cells take advantage of the same technology as their opposition. In particular, the organisation is assisted by the media, whose lust for sensationalism ensures that each attack is publicised to reach the widest constituency of al-Qaeda supporters.

The equation between the insurgent and the opposition prevails; in this case, a powerful and comprehensive opposition has ensured that only the most potent insurgent force can challenge it. The characteristics of the global insurgent begin to emerge. The defining condition becomes the international dispersal of the organisation, *not* the visible assets that are being destroyed in Afghanistan. Although in Sri Lanka Prabhakaran's assets have similar functions, they are limited by their ethnicity, which is Tamil, and their centre of gravity, which is a small area of Sri Lanka. Against a global counter-strategy, Prabhakaran could not survive in such a limited territorial and cultural space. Bin Laden, the global insurgent, has overcome both these problems by geographic dispersal and multi-ethnicity. The survival characteristic of the global insurgent organisation is its statelessness. To survive in this configuration, al-Qaeda exploits the freedoms and technologies that the current environment has to offer.

Organisation

Bin Laden was fortunate to have created his organisation before he was outlawed by the world's most powerful counter-insurgent forces. The preceding phases of his global manifestation, in which his activities were unopposed, if not tacitly condoned, by the West, allowed him freedom to travel and cultivate structures and contacts that he was to call on later. His support and operational structures grew in parallel during the same period, in three phases. When bin Laden arrived in Afghanistan, he found a leadership and organisational vacuum. In 1980, there were as many as 84 resistance groups based around Peshawar, all intent on fighting the Soviets in Afghanistan, but without a centre or a coordinating infrastructure. With his organising skills and capital, bin Laden was able to impose himself on the disparate *mujahideen* and create an effective order out of their chaotic presence. His plans were irresistible to the independent-minded fighters because he could deliver their missing ingredient, logistics. Bin Laden set up his first organising base, at that time named the Maktab al-Khidmat (MAK), in Peshawar. It was soon running like a business, with managers and accountants organising reception centres, training camps and procurement programmes.[92] His self-generated mission was now to recruit worldwide for the Afghanistan campaign, and recruiting offices were opened in more than 50 countries. The MAK paid the fighters, arranged their international travel and training and organised the supporting structures, including weapons supplies and logistic roads into Afghanistan. To meet these costs, bin Laden created a network of businesses, banks and benefactors.[93] When the Afghan campaign ended, the recruiting and manpower organising machinery (by then referred to as al-Qaeda) went into reverse cycle to disperse up to 22,000 surviving *mujahideen* veterans back to their countries of origin.[94] During the second phase of his international development, based in Sudan, bin Laden widened his capacity-building interest and al-Qaeda became the 'world bank' for Islamic insurgent forces.[95] Although his operational influence was secondary to the leaders of the local insurgent groups he supported, bin Laden maintained a prominent role through his provision of funds. His businesses and range of contacts continued to widen in order to fuel this effort. In his third organising phase, bin Laden moved back to his Afghanistan base. Although he was supportive of the Taliban, he had by this time already begun to capitalise on his overseas operational assets, using his massive reserve of mujahideen returnees as the basis of a cellular organisation. By now he had fashioned a formidable weapon. His mujahideen were, by their formative training and war experiences, a tested force. They were united through the al-Qaeda base and, despite their heterogeneous ethnicity, they trusted bin Laden; they were a brotherhood, which had come together in the crucible of the same war and had passed to and from Afghanistan through the same al-Qaeda system to return as legitimate citizens in their 50 different countries of origin. Now bin Laden was calling them in, not to support diverse local insurrections, but as instruments of his own attack on the West.

Bin Laden controls this asset in the manner of a corporate chief executive. His command system works best when it is concentrated in one safe base. His management technique is to delegate into functional areas. These operate individually and can also be separated in space, but their most successful manifestations have been in Jeddah, Sudan and Afghanistan prior to September 2001, when he could locate them together and move easily between them in a coordinating role. His chief functional areas are financial operations, military operations, media and information policy, legal/religious policy and political policy. He also has a highly effective travel and movements department.[96] Bin Laden's increasing awareness of hostile surveillance and US intrusion capabilities has forced him to erect organisational 'firewalls' between departments and between separate operations in the same department. This compartmentalisation is reproduced throughout his organisation to make it impossible to enter the system from the edge and gain a knowledge of the whole. The only point where the strands of his organisation come together is in bin Laden himself.

Financial operations
Bin Laden's unique contributions to his insurgent movement are

his business skills, his logistic management techniques and, above all, his ability to fund operations. During its strongest earning period, bin Laden's business and income-raising structures generated between $200m and $300m annually.[97] Many of bin Laden's financial sources are overt, including businesses, charities and contributions from wealthy benefactors. According to the US Central Intelligence Agency (CIA), almost one-fifth of all humanitarian NGOs operating globally are Islamic. Besides having a legitimate presence in every one of bin Laden's operational areas, Islamic NGOs disburse and receive more than a billion dollars annually.[98] Bin Laden's illegal sources of income include credit-card fraud, theft and the culture and export of heroin. When bin Laden returned to Afghanistan in the third phase of his career, Taliban leader Mullah Omar conceded to al-Qaeda's control areas of Nangarhur province, where the cultivation of heroin and the imposition of tax roadblocks provided a source of income to Afghanistan-based units.[99]

Bin Laden's operating principle has been to generate and disburse funds on a continuous basis. His banking network, which prior to September 2001 was internationally spread, controlled feeder and operational support accounts.[100] His support cells generate funds, and his more clandestine operational cells are responsible for their movement and final disbursement.[101] Bin Laden's logistic and financial interests also include a controlling interest in at least 23 merchant ships.[102]

Official sources and analysts disagree on the impact of US counter-insurgent efforts against bin Laden's sources of income. Peter Bergen's report on the May 2001 trial in New York of the Kenyan and Tanzanian embassy bombers indicates that bin Laden was crippled by cash shortages during his Sudan phase in the mid-1990s. However, the trial statements are at odds with Robinson's account of the same period in Sudan, as well as his descriptions of the establishment of the 'Brotherhood group' of 134 globally-deployed Arab businessmen, whose legitimate businesses allow them to transfer money routinely around the world.[103] According to the *Los Angeles Times*, despite freezing $80m and seizing $12.5m following September 2001, Rob Nichols, US Deputy Assistant Treasury Secretary, was unable to say what effect this had on the 'terrorists' financial lines'.[104] It is certain that all of bin Laden's traceable assets, including his income from drug-trafficking, have by now been shut down. However, it is also certain that a sizeable element of his fund-raising financial cells will continue to function whatever the outcome in Afghanistan. Bin Laden's current problem is how to transfer these assets from their overt and legal sources to his operational cells. Although he has couriers, the *hawalas* are likely to provide him with a better option. Several hundred *hawalas*, or individual traders, operate throughout the Middle East in an informal, paperless credit-transfer system, with a nucleus of traffic which runs between India, Pakistan and Dubai. Although bin Laden's financial capability is diminished and his flexibility for transferring cash restricted, there is likely to be a residual fund-raising capability in his surviving sources of income. This limitation should be set in the context of his greatly-reduced running costs after the collapse of his Afghanistan forces and the sobering statistic that future operations in the 11 September vein are not estimated to cost more than $200,000 each.[105]

The cells

Another source of bin Laden's strength that is likely to survive the post-September 2001 reprisals is his extensive international cell structure. The rash of media stories describing the arrests of apparent sleeper cells in several countries give the misleading impression that these actions may have diminished al-Qaeda's international capability. This is unlikely to be the case; even if only half of the core of 15,000–20,000 mujahideen fighters who returned from the Afghanistan campaign to their own countries in the 1990s are still active supporters, that is vastly more than the number that have been arrested or are needed to continue bin Laden's tasks. Moreover, al-Qaeda has, in most of its 63 feeder countries, continued to expand, rather than contract.

The survivability of an insurgent cell lies in its concealment and its ability to live inconspicuously. In France, Germany and the UK, al-Qaeda recruiters have been extremely successful at targeting the Muslim population, and at penetrating a potential supporter's veneer of success and stability to find 'the embers of a lingering fury at perceived discrimination inflicted by the population of the host state'.[106] Ouassini Cherifi, a first-generation Frenchman, 'was a model of integration and upward mobility', with a degree in mathematics and a job as a receptionist in an international hotel chain near Paris. But recruiters discovered the intensity of his feelings against the Western lifestyle and exploited his concealed ambitions for revenge, even martyrdom, by successfully recruiting him to be a logistic organiser in the European support cell.[107] In Malaysia and Singapore, the structure of Muslim religious meeting groups was successfully penetrated and radicalised by travelling Indonesian clerics who moved freely as teachers from state to state. After cultivating the cells, the US Embassy and UK High Commission in Singapore were selected as targets for attack and carefully reconnoitred with videos of likely sites for truck bombs. At this stage, senior al-Qaeda officials arrived by air to supervise and coach the local group (of middle managers, electrical engineers, shopkeepers and a condominium manager who provided the venue for the meetings) through the final stages of the operation. Al-Qaeda's policy towards the survival of an activated cell is ruthless. While every effort is made to save and extract the core operations staff, who only visit at the final stages of preparation, the local members of a group will be left to face almost certain capture. In the Singapore plot and the Tanzanian embassy bombing, the core al-Qaeda operatives left the state using a well-organised escape plan, but the local supporters, who had risked everything to film the targets, hire the vans, purchase the chemicals and assemble the bombs, were virtually 'hung out to dry'.[108]

Operations

Al-Qaeda fighters could be described as formidable but fallible in their operations. Their organisation is pervasive and well-established, so that it can survive many setbacks; attacks are boldly conceived and, when they succeed, capture public attention to an unprecedented degree. Counter-measures to protect likely targets are over-stretched and may fail again because they are premised on a Western perception of the attacker which is evidently incorrect. The al-Qaeda fighter is by motivation a true soldier, prepared to stand and fight to the death for an idea. The temporal attractions of survival and the rewards of looting and unlicensed behaviour are ruled out by the fundamentalist nature of their motivation. The al-Qaeda attacker is determined and in most cases ready to die in the execution of a mission. Nevertheless, at the lowest level not only are the fighters likely to be the weakest point in the organis- ation, but they are evidently considered to be expendable by the top level of the al-Qaeda organisation.

As a military unit, bin Laden's veterans have only served together in Afghanistan, where their cohesion was never seriously challenged by the Northern Alliance. With the sudden arrival of Western forces, their collapse was immediate and they reverted to guerrilla tactics. Their success therefore has been as a globally-dis- persed organisation. Nevertheless, even in this manifestation they lack continuity of experience. The core operators who moved around internationally to assist local cells have been highly effec- tive, but the local element were more fallible and in some cases made important mistakes which compromised the full impact of their mission.

Until September 2001, al-Qaeda continued to recruit and train. By now the Afghanistan training camps have been disman- tled, although smaller local groups may continue to meet in uncontrolled areas of Kashmir, Pakistan, Somalia and northern Yemen.[109] Closer to the West, radical cells may continue to meet and possibly train among Muslim migrant communities.[110] Aside from the logistic effort involved in moving its recruits through Pakistan to the Afghanistan training camps, the actual training regime, once they arrive, is similar to the LTTE's. Al-Qaeda has at least one, very comprehensive, training manual and makes full use of videos for training as well as operations.[111] As in the case of the LTTE, al-Qaeda fighters are taught to shoot to kill, and in most cases can handle their weapons and equipment effectively.

What are bin Laden's military objectives? Are they linked to a political manifesto? Before bin Laden reorganised to anticipate the consequences of the September 2001 attacks, his forces were organised for two different contingencies: operations as field units in Afghanistan and operations as individual cells. The former contingency failed after the arrival of US and other Western forces, but al-Qaeda's most spectacular successes have in any case been in the latter manifestation. During the Cold War, analysts maintained that an insurrection culminated at the seizure of the levers of power within the state.[112] This view stressed the importance of key targets that rebels would have to capture to gain control.[113] Against a democratic system these objectives are less relevant; in the case of a popular insurgency, the government may be prevailed upon to make concessions, and may even be forced out of power by a demoralised electorate that has been caught up in the insurgent campaign for too long. A prolonged campaign of violent propaganda erodes the credibility of the government and makes life for the population seem unbearable. Bin Laden's targets in the West suggest a campaign that employs the 'propaganda of the deed'. His intent is assisted by a Western counter-strategy that isolates migrant Muslim communities and globally continues to exacerbate their feelings of exclusion and discrimination.

Despite the narrowness of the data base, the purpose of this section is not to analyse a particular campaign but to emphasise that a globally-organised insurgent force can survive by using the West's own technology, individual freedoms and media. Like the Lumpen insurgent commander, bin Laden is also a virus of his environment, although his manifestation is quite different. Global change has made democratic government more vulnerable to violent propaganda; the tragedy for poor and excluded communities as well as ordinary citizens, the targets and the front-line soldiers of an insurgent campaign, is that a successful culmination is becoming more and more difficult for either side to achieve.

Conclusion

The central proposition of this paper is that global changes have altered the nature of insurgency by weakening some governments, and empowering the forces that seek to overthrow them. Not all states involved in counter-insurgency are weakened by globalisation; insurgents face both rich and poor governments, whose wealth, democratic development and military power have a direct bearing on the organisation and tactics of rebel forces. A state that is weakened by global change provides an environment in which a poorly-constituted insurgent force can survive. Because the government is unable to dominate its territory and population, insurgent forces move freely, and can be less militarily capable. Insurgents in a weak state are able to raise funds more easily by pillaging the state's resources and trading them on to international markets. Insurgents who struggle against rich and militarily-powerful governments have to be better organised and operate in a more effective manner. In many cases, they will have to raise an operating income through their supporting constituency. The possibility of making huge sums of money from resource trading in weak states exposes a movement to the temptations of making violence a way of life, as opposed to being a means to achieve a long-term revolutionary goal. In view of the opportunities for gaining personal wealth and for self-aggrandisement, a more precise understanding of the insurgent leader's organisation may lead to a better interpretation of their real intent. It is important to know whether insurgents are warlords or genuine revolutionaries, and whether their individual followers are true soldiers motivated by a higher cause, or real warriors motivated by personal gain.

Warlords or revolutionaries?

Each of the four types of insurgent force described in this paper uses illegal methods to acquire funds. These may include the extraction of natural resources, raising revenues from existing commercial and agricultural activities in their area of control, raiding state facilities (banks, armouries and storage depots) and protracted criminal activities such as piracy, extortion and smuggling. It is sometimes hard to decide whether an insurgent movement is engaging in warlordism or in a genuine revolutionary campaign. By definition, a warlord regime is purely extractive. Faction leaders who are not warlords exercise a social responsibility towards their constituent population which, at a minimum, means providing a degree of personal security and developing or supporting the essential conditions for their livelihood. Warlordism by contrast is a strictly negative presence that implies extortion, racketeering and the interception of revenues that normally belong to a state, without any mitigating social obligations or the provision of security for the local population. An insurgent movement becomes a warlord faction when it is unable to translate military success into any form of social or political responsibility that benefits the population.

The warlord is a virus of the post-Cold War strategic era; he is responding to an environment and profiting from it, but unlike the revolutionary is not trying to change it. A warlord is not a mindless barbarian striving to return an ungovernable population to its ancient tribal divisions; rather, his logic and motivation are entirely modern. He seeks to exploit a global market and a vulnerable society for personal gain. The sums of money involved compare with the income of an international corporation. The profits from the success of commercial operations are used to sustain the military capabilities of the faction, but the proportion of banked assets that goes towards maintaining a lifestyle would indicate that this, and not the desire for political change, is the warlord's driving motivation. A warlord may articulate a credo which has the appearance of a long-term political goal, but the manifesto is seldom developed as an ideology or as a motive for campaigning. In practical terms, the day-to-day military activities of the faction do not relate to the achievement of a long-term political aim. A warlord organisation is also distinguished by its lack of genuine structures for husbanding and canvassing popular support. Warlords do not need or care about people and will ignore, and even exploit, a population's humanitarian needs.

A genuine revolutionary movement may use the same fund-raising techniques as the warlord. The distinction is that, at the culmination of the campaign, a revolutionary movement will have to prepare itself to govern the population, hopefully through a democratic process of selection. A genuine revolutionary movement that has maintained a close relationship with its supporting population is more likely to accept a democratic transfer of power, and also more likely to succeed in winning the resulting election. A warlord organisation by contrast will resist a successful peace process. A re-establishment of a monopoly of power within the state and the consequent imposition of law and order challenges the warlord's *modus vivendi*.

It is possible for each category of insurgent movement to succumb to the attractions of warlordism and abandon its revolutionary aim. However, Lumpen and clan forces are more likely than popular and global forces to operate as warlord factions. The latter categories can rely less on pillaging the resources of a weak state, and therefore have to develop income-raising strategies that involve the cooperation of a population. Thus, they cannot afford to lose its support.

Real warriors or true soldiers?

One of the most important distinguishing features of an insurgent force is how and why its followers fight. In the four categories described in this paper, some fight in a ritualistic manner, which seems to indicate that they wish to drive off their opponents but not necessarily to kill them, particularly if doing so risks a dangerous confrontation. Others attack deliberately in order to destroy their enemy, and will face hazards, even death, to achieve this. It is helpful for security forces to know which type of insurgent fighter they are opposing. This paper concludes that in each of the

four typologies, two categories of fighter can be found: real warriors and true soldiers. This assessment methodology originates
from Keegan's perception of soldiers in a field army, and is
adapted to explain a similar distinction in insurgent forces.[1] The
organisation of an insurgent force and its actual, as opposed to
apparent, motivation are the determinants of whether an insurgent
is a real warrior, or a true soldier.

Real warriors are found in a movement or fighting unit that
is informally structured, and characterised by a horizontal organisation in which a leader has a loose control over a number of
sub-units. Junior commanders therefore have to be self-reliant.
Their authority rests on having a physical presence, instilling fear
and acting with immediate brutality towards any signs of dissent.
The real warrior in this unit fights for personal gain. A successful
action brings immediate reward: loot, food, drugs, alcohol, rest and
good living for days, possibly weeks. Conversely, failure leads to
continued deprivation of all these things, and the prospect of
further discomfort and danger before they can be regained. Except
in a perfunctory manner, real warriors are not trained or motivated
by the unit they fight for. They have not been taught to put an
ideological cause above their own safety and comfort, so that when
they attack they do so for personal gain. They are less concerned
with destroying the enemy than with the prize of the objective, and
will usually fight so as to drive the enemy away, rather than risk
a destructive confrontation. During fighting their instincts for
self-preservation are not suppressed, and will overwhelm the need
to press home a contested action. A real warrior is nevertheless
capable of fighting tenaciously for a key objective that has a life- or
livelihood-threatening significance.

A true soldier is the antithesis of a real warrior. True soldiers
are the consequence of a strongly-organised, vertically-structured
organisation in which junior commanders are appointed and therefore empowered by the movement, and less by their domineering
presence. The true soldier's behaviour is conditioned by training,
motivation and a degree of relative value deprivation. A true
soldier also has greater choice as to whether to join the movement,
and is a volunteer to a much greater degree than the real warrior.
True soldiers tend not to join a movement for personal gain

because in most cases the prospects for looting are limited. They are formally trained in military techniques, in particular shooting to kill. They are also taught to put the cause firmly above their personal needs. When true soldiers fight, success does not alter their lives; after the successful attack there is no prospect of booty or rapine. Any useful or valuable goods that are seized are recovered for the group, not for the individual. True soldiers are therefore fighting for a higher reason, and are forced to suspend their instincts for self-preservation and press home an attack even when the opposition is effective. As a rule, an attack is carefully planned to ensure success. True soldiers are therefore similar to regular troops in the defence forces of a democratic state.

Within an insurgent sub-unit there will tend to be a homogeneity of either real warriors or true soldiers. But at a higher level, a movement may comprise a mix of fighting units, some of which have a distinctly warrior approach to combat, and some with a true soldier approach. Generally, Lumpen forces are more likely to comprise warriors, and popular forces more likely to comprise true soldiers. The circumstances of each unit, its training, leadership and motivation, are a more reliable guide as to the nature of its fighters.

Globalisation and insurgency

Insurgent behaviour is influenced by the environment of the host state and the strength of the opposition forces. By adding an assessment of these conditions to each insurgent force's organisation, *modus operandi* and support arrangements, four distinct categories emerge.

Lumpen forces are a response to a weak-state environment. Movements are horizontally organised and the command linkages between fighting units are fragile, encouraging disloyalty and opportunism among junior commanders. Individual fighters tend by disposition to be selfishly motivated. Forces are militarily weak, with a local operating range. Lumpen movements tend to be in the warlord category.

Clan forces are in some respects similar to Lumpen forces, with the important distinction that their organisation is based on family groups that are related to a particular clan or tribe. This

Chart 1 Distinguishing features in insurgent forces

	Lumpen	Clan	Popular	Global
Motivation	Individual Gain			Collective Gain
Opposition forces	Weak			Strong
Organisation structures	Horizontal			Vertical
Training	Casual			Organised
Recruiting	Near-compulsion			Voluntary
International structures	Undeveloped			Very developed

makes them militarily more formidable and gives them a significant, long-term survivability. The clan's traditional structures are threatened by more successful metropolitan and commercially-oriented societies.

Popular insurgent forces are a response to a stronger state in which the insurgent has less freedom of movement, and needs to be better organised. Popular forces have vertical structures, which have developed international elements as well as effective organisations for mobilising popular support. Individual followers are comparatively well-educated, motivated and formally trained as fighters. By disposition, they are true soldiers. The force is militarily competent, with an international reach. Popular leaders do not tend to be warlords.

Global insurgent forces are in some respects similar to popular forces, except that their revolutionary objectives are wider than the overthrow of the regime of a particular state. The global insurgent is organised to survive in an international environment using several supporting populations in different countries. The global insurgent has an international reach, and relies on the visibility of the deed rather than the practical consequences of its impact. These characteristics are summarised in Chart 1.

It is important to stress that this typology does not intend to fit a real-life movement precisely. Because the RUF is used to illustrate some aspects of the Lumpen force, it does not mean that the RUF is regarded as having a wholly Lumpen character. The typology is intended as an indicator, and it would be more accurate to say that the RUF has a Lumpen tendency, and some popular-force characteristics. A real-life insurgent movement can be explained and defined by applying the relevant characteristics from each model.

It should be stressed again that not all insurgent movements should be seen as negative forces which have to be opposed. In future, however, insurgencies that challenge an internationally-supported peace process may find themselves the legitimate target of a counter-insurgency campaign.

Doctrine and military planning

The doctrine writer and the military planner need to know the nature of the adversary in order to prepare for a campaign. Although these models are no more than a first step towards conceptualising insurgent forces, even in this rudimentary form they raise several issues for planners and leaders of future international interventions.

A wider span of counter-insurgent responses

The consequence of globalisation is that insurgencies now manifest themselves in several distinct forms, not as variations of the same form. The response to each is characterised by different planning assumptions, different principles and a different approach. The focus of a response to a Lumpen force is essentially local, but a campaign against a popular force would include some international objectives. Planners' assumptions about the reactions of fighters of one category would be dangerously wrong if applied to other categories. Intervening forces have to protect themselves in a different way for each contingency. The geographic range and character of the response to each type is as distinct as the insurgent forces that define it. This diversity is not reflected in current doctrine.

The globalisation of counter-insurgency

Cold War-era counter-insurgency doctrines addressed insurgent forces that were seeking to overthrow the government or regime of a particular state. As a result, counter-insurgency thinking is essentially national in character. There have been no wider efforts to create an international approach, as there has been in the case of peacekeeping techniques. The globalisation of insurgency leads inexorably to the globalisation of counter-insurgency.[2]

New doctrine

Existing counter-insurgent doctrine, despite in some cases being published after the end of the Cold War, is a revised version of a national approach. A new doctrine arising from an appraisal of current insurgent manifestations will have to be:

- internationally recognised;
- interdisciplinary in its approach; and
- multi-layered, addressing the local situation as well as related activities at sub-regional and international level.

Coordination not cooperation

The need for a concerted approach towards restoring security and government in a conflict area, and in some cases far beyond it, contradicts the current independence of each responding agency and organisation in an international response. A new approach will demand that governments that pay for development and relief efforts associated with a counter-insurgent intervention will increasingly dictate how it is to be coordinated as part of a single strategic aim.

Appendices

Appendix 1 Table of Somali factions and forces (as at August 2001)

Clan/Family	Faction leader	Political affiliations	No. of fighters	Support weapon	Notes
Issak*	Mohamed Ibrahim Egal	Somaliland government	10,000 troops	T64 MBT, 105mm	Police force 300, public radio/TV
Habargidir/Saad	Hussein Aideed	USC/SNA + Aideed	200	18 technicals, 122mm	Public radio
Habargidir/Saad	Osman Atto	USC/SNA + Atto	150	8 technicals	Public radio
Muthsade	Mohamed Qanyare	USC	300–400	40 technicals	
Majerten	Mohamed Said Hersi Morgan	SPM	900 +	12 technicals	Arrested by Ethiopians
Abgael	Mussa Sudi Yallohow		1,200–1,500	30 technicals, med. arty 120mm MOR, 40mmAA	
Rahenwein	Shari Gadud	RRA	200–300	50 technicals	Trained by Ethiopians, public radio
Marehan	General Ahmed Warsome	SNF + K. Alliance	200	18 technicals	Trained + supported by Mogadishu businessmen and Shari'a courts
Marehan	Colonel Bihi	SNF	800	30 technicals	
Majerten	Abdulatin Yussuf	SSDF (Puntland President)	800–1,500	T62, T54 MBT, lt. Arty 15–25 technicals	+ secret police
Marehan	Colonel Barre Hirraleh	SNF + K. Alliance	1,000–2,000	30 technicals	
Ayr Habargidir	Serrar	K. Alliance			In hospital
Ayr	Mohammed Dhere	SRRC	300	18 technicals	

Notes

* Head of state

1. Potentially all male members of a clan can be armed, so strengths vary on a day-to-day basis.

2. Sub-elements of a clan may alter political affiliation.

3. This chart is illustrative only; strengths and affiliations have changed since August 2001.

Source: Compiled by James Foster from interviews with UN Security Staff.

Appendix 2 Select list of insurgent-group websites

Group	URL	Updated	Languages	Overview of contents
Northern Alliance Afghanistan	www.payamemujahid .com	Regularly	English Pashto Dari	Site produced by 'Afghan Mujahideen Publications'. Only the home page in English. Notable features: weekly-updated online version of the Payam-e-Mujahid newsletter; 'Radio Voice of Mujahid' online.
Taliban Afghanistan	www.afghanistan-ie.com	9/01	English Pashto Dari	The former official site of the 'Islamic Emirate of Afghanistan' included interviews and the 'Voice of Sharia' radio station. Shut down by its Pakistan-based ISP shortly after 11 September.
Hezb-e-Islami Afghanistan	www.hezb-e-islami.org	Regularly	English Dari Pashto	Hezb-e-Islami's proposed legislative reforms and economic and foreign policies, though these date from before the fall of the Taliban. Articles on the overthrow of the communist government in 1992 and the role of women in an Islamic society.
UNITA Angola	www.unita.org	3/12/01	Portuguese English	The official website of the UNITA political party, with aims and objectives. Represents 'the new Leadership of UNITA under Eugenio Manuvakola' and distances itself from Jonas Savimbi and his actions since the late 1970s.
CNDD/FDD Burundi	www.burundi-info.com	Regularly	French English Kirundi Kiswahili	Site contains CNDD/FDD statements, reports from international news agencies and some local newspapers. Much of the content is only available on the French-language version.
ELN Colombia	www.web.net/eln www.eln-voces.com	Regularly Regularly	English Spanish	The ELN's website has separate English- and Spanish-language versions. Both contain details of the group's aims and objectives, history, interviews with ELN commanders and criticism of the US and Colombian governments' anti-drug policies.

Group / Country	URL	Date / frequency	Language(s)	Description
FARC Colombia	www.farc-ep.org	16/11/01	Spanish English	The official FARC website contains details of the group's history, aims and objectives. The bi-monthly newsletter 'Resistencia' is also available on the site.
RCD-Goma DRC	www.congo.co.za	Regularly	English French	The official site of the RCD-Goma. Contains details of the group's aims and objectives, along with news articles and RCD-Goma press releases. The majority of the site is only available in English.
RCD-ML DRC	www.congorcd.org	5/12/01	English French	The official site of the RCD-ML (RCD/Kisangani). Contains a useful collection of statements and documents from the RCD-ML leadership, notably the statements regarding the faction's merger with the MLC.
MLC DRC	www.managingbusiness.com/mlc	Regularly	French English	Belgian-based MLC site. Contains news, statements and press releases from the MLC. The majority of the site is only available in French.
ELF Eritrea	http://users.erols.com/meskerem	Unknown	English Arabic Tigrinya	US-based site of the Alliance of Eritrean National Forces. Contains articles, reports from international news agencies and the quarterly ELF-RC international newsletter.
Harkat ul-Mujahideen India	www.ummah.net.pk/harkat	Unknown	English	Pakistan-based site providing information on the group's activities in Kashmir, several articles on *jihad* and Kashmir-related internet links. Much of the site is still under construction.
Komalah Iran	www.komalah.org	Regularly	Kurdish Farsi English	Komalah's official site outlines the group's aims and objectives, including some details of its activities in Iraqi Kurdistan.
KDP Iraq	www.kdp.pp.se	Regularly	English	The official KDP international site, based in Sweden. Contains sections on the KDP's aims, objectives and history, including events in Northern Iraq during/after the Iran–Iraq and Gulf Wars. Also has sections on the geography and culture of Kurdistan.

Group/Country	URL	Updated	Language	Description
PUK Iraq	www.puk.org	Regularly	English Kurdish	The official PUK website, with information on the group's history, aims and objectives. Useful documents section includes transcripts of speeches by PUK leader Jalal Talibani, reports from the Kurdish regional government and KDP-PUK agreements.
Hizbollah Lebanon	www.hizbollah.org	22/10/01	English Arabic	The official Hizbollah site, contains information on the group's origins and current activities, along with speeches, statements and press reports.
Hamas Palestine	www.palestine-info.org/ arabic/hamas/index.htm www.palestine-info.org/ /hamas/index.htm	Regularly Regularly	Arabic English	The official Hamas site, with information on the group's history, aims and objectives. Also contains biographies of *Hamas* leaders, an archive of press releases and responses to newspaper reports. Several sections in the Arabic version of the site are more extensive and up-to-date than the English version.
PFLP Palestine	www.pflp-pal.org	Regularly	English	The official website of the PFLP political party, with information on the group's origins, political aims and objectives. Unlike the Hamas site, it does not mention the group's paramilitary activities.
RUF Sierra Leone	www.rufp.org	Regularly	English	Official website of the Revolutionary United Front Party, contains a mission statement, details of the RUF's history and aims, documents, agreements and photos. Also contains press releases and responses to newspaper articles.
LTTE Sri Lanka	www.eelam.com	Regularly	English Tamil	The LTTE's official site, contains press releases and information on the group's aims and objectives. Some sections of the site are available in Tamil.
Republican Sinn Fein United Kingdom	http://free.freespeech.org /republicansf/intro.htm	Regularly	English	Official site of the RSF party gives details of the organisation's aims, objectives and proposals for the future administration of Ireland. The party denies reported links with the CIRA and RIRA, and there is no mention of either group's paramilitary activities.

Source: Compiled by James Foster.

Notes

Acknowledgements

This paper could not have been researched in Colombo, Nairobi and Freetown without the help and hospitality of correspondents, military staff, senior UN officials, civil police, government officials and the brave and long suffering individuals who have had to support or be part of insurgent forces. I also wish to thank Mats Berdal and his colleagues for their excellent advice on my earlier drafts and the British Academy for encouraging me to take on this project with their assistance.

Introduction

1. UK Ministry of Defence (MoD), 'Notes on the Fantasian Army', *Army Code No: 70737* (London: Her Majesty's Stationery Office (HMSO), 1972).
2. UK MoD, 'Counter-Revolutionary Operations', in *Land Operations Part 2. Army Code No. 70516* (London: MoD, 1969); UK MoD, 'Counter Revolutionary Operations', in *Land Operations Vol. III. Part 1. General Principles. Army Code No. 70516* (London: MoD, 1977); Chief of General Staff, 'Counter Insurgency Operations', in *Army Field Manual Vol. 5. Operations Other Than War. Army Code 71596* (London: MoD, 1995).
3. UK Chiefs of Staff, *Peace Support Operations*, Joint Warfare Publication 3–50 (London: MoD, 1996); Swedish Armed Forces, *Peace Support Operations* (Stockholm: MSK ToD, 1997).
4. UK MoD, *Wider Peacekeeping* (London: HMSO, 1994); *Peace Support Operations*, Joint Warfare Publication 3–50; US Department of the Army, *FM100–23; Peace Operations* (Washington DC: Department of the Army, 1994).
5. 'Counter Insurgency Operations', p. 1.
6. Sir Michael Howard, 'Mistake To Declare This a "War"', *RUSI Journal*, December 2001, p. 1

Chapter 1

1. Mary Kaldor was among the first to put these developments into perspective. See Mary Kaldor, *New and Old Wars: Organised Violence in a Global Era* (Cambridge, MA: Polity Press, 1999).

2 David Harvey shows that improving the speed of ships and land transport had been 'compressing the world' since 1850. David Harvey, *Conditions of Post Modernity* (Oxford: Blackwell, 1989), cited in Ankie Hoogvelt (ed.), *Globalisation and the Post Colonial World*, second edition (London: Palgrave, 2001). Mark Duffield has argued that the 'exclusion of the south' can be traced to the 1970s. Mark Duffield, *Global Governance and the New Wars* (London: Zed Books, 2001), Chapter 1.

3 David Held and Anthony McGrew, with David Goldblatt and Jonathan Perraton, 'Globalisation', *Global Governance*, vol. 5, no. 4, 1999, pp. 483–96.

4 Jean-Christophe Rufin, 'The Economics of War: A New Theory for Armed Conflicts', *Forum*, Series 2 (Geneva: International Committee of the Red Cross, February 2000).

5 *Ibid.*

6 In a Maoist insurgency, 'wilderness areas' referred to an extensive refuge so wild that the technical and numerical advantages of government forces were greatly reduced, and combat would therefore be on the insurgent's terms.

7 Harvey, *Conditions of Post Modernity*, cited in Hoogvelt (ed.), *Globalisation and the Post Colonial World*.

8 Interview with Karen Davies, Nairobi, 9 August 2001. Davies was one of a small group of correspondents that followed Kabila's campaign in 1997.

9 From information supplied by Paul Molinaro, Department of Defence Management and Security Analysis, Cranfield University, 6 August 2001.

10 The cost of container traffic is dictated by the popularity of the route. A 'heavy leg', for example exporting Western goods to the Gulf and Sub-Saharan Africa, is heavily subscribed and therefore operating at cost, whereas the returning or 'light' leg, in which many containers would be empty, would offer transportation at less than cost. This favoured small entrepreneurs seeking to export on the light legs.

11 'The Perils of Packet Switching', *The Economist*, 6 April 2002, p. 13.

12 Interview with David Hall, 6 January 2002. Hall is a consultant and former vice-president of several container-shipping lines.

13 In West African crisis zones, small-scale foreign traders, who in some cases had been operating in the region for several decades, acted as intermediaries between the international market and local dealers. They exploited the proliferation of communications and transport as well as the deregulation of local resource markets, which could not be controlled by international sanctions.

14 Frances Cairncross, *The Death of Distance 2.0: How the Communications Revolution Will Change Our Lives* (London: Texere Publishing, 2001).

15 Some 150,000 kilometres of overland and submarine cables linked distant British colonies with a central administration. *Ibid.*, p. 25.

16 *Ibid.*, p. 3.

17 Michael Skapinker, 'The Tongue Twisters', *Financial Times*, 28 December 2000, cited in Cairncross, *The Death of Distance*, p. 280.

18 *Ibid.*

19 *Ibid.*, p. 215.

20 In David Harvey's description of hedge-fund dealing, the tiny profits in each transaction would not in normal circumstances have

been worth picking up. However, with computer-assisted data processing money could now be made from 'gathering up infinitesimally fractional differences in the movement in prices'. Harvey, *Conditions of Post Modernity*, cited in Hoogvelt (ed.), *Globalisation and the Post Colonial World*.

21 A. Sampson, *The Midas Touch: Money, People and Power from the East to the West* (London: Hodder and Stoughton, 1989), cited in Hoogvelt (ed.), *Globalisation and the Post Colonial World*, p. 88.

22 *Ibid.*

23 Hoogvelt (ed.), *Globalisation and the Post Colonial World*, p. 175.

24 Eric Hobsbawm, *Age of Extremes* (London: Abacus, 1997), pp. 422–26.

25 Editorial, *The Observer*, 2 January 2000, p. 24.

26 Paul Kennedy, 'Preparing for the 21st Century: Winners and Losers', *New York Review of Books*, 11 February 1993, cited in Patrick O'Meara, Howard Mehliinger and Matthew Krain (eds), *Globalisation and the Challenges of a New Century: A Reader* (Bloomington, IN: Indiana University Press, 2000).

27 Eugene Linden, 'Exploding Cities of the Developing World', *Foreign Affairs*, vol. 75, no. 1, 1996, cited in O'Meara, Mehliinger and Krain (eds), *Globalisation*.

28 *Ibid.*

29 Peter Marcuse and Ronald van Kempen, *Globalising Cities: A New Spatial Order* (Oxford: Blackwell, 2000), p. 271.

30 Linden, 'Exploding Cities', cited in O'Meara, Mehliinger and Krain (eds), *Globalisation*, p. 411.

31 Held *et al.*, 'Globalisation', p. 486.

32 Benjamin Barber, 'Jihad vs McWorld', *Atlantic Monthly*, March 1992, cited in O'Meara, Mehliinger and Krain (eds), *Globalisation*.

33 Kaldor, *New and Old Wars*, p. 77.

34 Much of this account is from Lieutenant-Colonel Joe Poraj-Wilczynski, UK Defence Advisor, British High Commission, Freetown. Interview, September 2001.

35 Tupac Shakur made records under the name 2Pac. His lyrics were nihilistic, rebellious, anti-authoritarian, sentimental and very violent. Interview with Mansel Fletcher, arts correspondent, 1 February 2002.

36 By the 1990s, one-third of Sub-Saharan African states were unable to exercise authority over their rural regions, or carry out public policies throughout their national territories. Joshua Forrest, 'State Inversion and Non-state Politics', in Leonardo Villalon and Phillip Huxtable (eds), *The African State at a Critical Juncture* (Boulder, CO: Lynne Rienner, 1998), p. 45.

37 The 'economies of civil war' has become a phenomenon, with its own genre of literature and research. See David Keen, *The Economic Functions of Violence in Civil Wars*, Adelphi Paper 320 (Oxford: Oxford University Press for the IISS, 1998); Duffield, *Global Governance and the New Wars*; William Reno, *Warlord Politics and African States* (Boulder, CO: Lynne Rienner, 1998); Mats Berdal and David Malone (eds), *Greed and Grievance: Economic Agendas in Civil Wars* (Boulder, CO: Lynne Rienner, 2000); Jakkie Cilliers and Peggy Mason (eds), *Peace, Profit or Plunder?* (Pretoria: Institute for Security Studies, 1999).

Chapter 2

1 When attempts to deliver anthrax spores through the US postal service succeeded in October 2001, public life in the US was immobilised by the population's

reactions, to a degree that probably exceeded the perpetrators' expectations.

2 For example, in Northern Ireland the UK government was, in the long term, strong enough to make compromises with republican leaders Gerry Adams and Martin McGuiness, which although alienating an element of Protestant support, has had the more powerful effect of isolating the remaining active insurgents from the vast majority of Catholics.

3 UK Chief of General Staff, 'Counter Insurgency Operations', pp. 5-2–5-4. See also Ian Beckett and John Pimlott (eds), *Armed Forces and Modern Counter-Insurgency* (London: St Martin's Press, 1985), esp. p. 33 on the British experience of local government in Dhofar, Oman, in the 1960s and 1970s.

4 This was particularly true of high-rise districts (such as Kowloon in Hong Kong), where the mass of people already on the streets can be rapidly augmented by the evacuation of buildings to outnumber and cut off a police riot squad.

5 In the Beirut attack, on 23 October 1983, 241 US Marines and 59 French soldiers were killed. See John Mackinlay, *The Peacekeepers* (London: Unwin Hyman, 1985), p. 85; and *Report of Commission on Beirut International Airport, 20 December 1983* (Washington DC: US Department of Defense, 1983). For a full description of the Nairobi attack, see Adam Robinson, *Bin Laden: Behind the Mask of the Terrorist* (Edinburgh: Mainstream, 2001), Chapter 17.

6 In December 2001, Northern Alliance forces, with US and British assistance, isolated Taliban forces in the Tora Bora complex using massive stand-off weapons. During the Soviet occupation of Afghanistan, this complex was not taken.

7 Both UNITA and the NPFL had guest houses at Jamba and Gbarnger, respectively. Abiodun Alao, John Mackinlay and Funmi Olonsakin, *Peacekeepers, Politicians, and Warlords: The Liberian Peace Process* (Tokyo: United Nations University, 1999), p. 44.

8 Christopher Clapham, 'Analysing African Insurgencies', in Clapham (ed.), *African Guerillas* (Oxford: James Currey, 1998), p. 11.

9 Alao *et al.*, *Peacekeepers, Politicians, and Warlords*, pp. 13–15.

10 A. Labrousse, *The Tupamaros* (London: Penguin, 1970), p. 15.

11 John Keegan, *A History of Warfare* (London: Hutchison, 1993), p. 213.

12 A. Hyman, *Afghanistan Under Soviet Domination 1964–83* (London: Macmillan, 1982), p. 21.

13 The Holy Spirit Movement (HSM) was essentially a spiritual response to widespread degeneration. Alice Lakwena's fighters were first of all required to submit themselves to a cleansing process, 'Holy Spirit Safety Precautions'. This ceremony, and strict prohibitions on looting, sex, smoking and alcohol, purported to ensure the safety of her followers. When they were killed or injured in the course of conflict, this was explained as proof of their failure to keep to the Holy Spirit Safety Precautions. H. Behrend, 'War in Northern Uganda: The Holy Spirit Movements of Alice Lakwena, Severino Lukoya and Joseph Kony (1986–1997)', in Clapham (ed.), *African Guerillas*.

14 Stephen Ellis, 'Liberia's Warlord Insurgency', in *ibid.*, p. 170. 'RUF Kills and Eats Dennis Mingo ... they ate his liver,

private parts and his heart. The rebels believe that if you eat your enemy's body if gives you supernatural powers and protects you from any curse arising from his death'. From the lead story of *PEEP*, 24 August 2001.

[15] Keegan, *A History of Warfare*, pp. 16 and 29. Keegan maintains that Shaka was not influenced by Europeans in his regimental organisation.

[16] *Ibid.*, pp. 54 and 55.

[17] Clapham, 'Analysing African Insurgencies', p. 9.

[18] M. R. Narayan Swamy, *Tigers of Lanka* (New Delhi: Rashtra Rachna Printers, 1994), Chapter 4.

[19] Alao *et al.*, *Peacekeepers, Politicians, and Warlords*, p. 21.

[20] Interview with Gibril Foday-Mussa of the Talking Drum Studio, Freetown, August 2001. Foday-Mussa was a cadre at the Matabh Ideological Centre.

[21] Keen, *The Economic Functions of Violence in Civil Wars*.

Chapter 3

[1] Clapham, 'Analysing African Insurgencies', pp. 6–7.

[2] UK Chief of General Staff, 'Counter Insurgency Operations', pp. 1–4 and 1–5.

[3] Keen, *The Economic Functions of Violence in Civil Wars*.

[4] Interview with UN officials and Diane De Guzman, a legal consultant and former humanitarian-agency executive, Nairobi, August 2001.

[5] In the case of the SPLA, the Sudan Relief and Rehabilitation Association (SRRA) acts as the liaison wing to oversee the movement of relief. UN officials confirm that relief stores flown into southern Sudan are 'reallocated' directly after issue to the SPLA logistic organisers, and a bare minimum is returned to civilian recipients. See also Mark Duffield, 'Post-Modern Conflict, Warlords, Post-Adjustment States and Private Protection', *Journal of Civil Wars*, April 1998.

[6] Lawrence Freedman, 'The Third World War', *Survival*, vol. 43, no. 4, Winter 2001–2002, p. 73.

[7] Steven Simon and Daniel Benjamin, 'The Terror', *ibid.*, p. 5.

[8] Jonathan Stevenson, 'Pragmatic Counter-Terrorism', *ibid.*, p. 35.

[9] Although British doctrine identifies seven different insurgent types, there is only one prescriptive doctrine for them all.

[10] The manual which supersedes the UK counter-insurgency doctrine of the 1980s and 1990s no longer contains the chapters defining and describing insurgency. Compare UK MoD, 'Counter Insurgency Operations' with its successor, *Tactical Handbook for Operations Other than War* (London: HMSO, December 1998).

[11] Keen, *The Economic Functions of Violence in Civil Wars*.

[12] Ibrahim Abdullah and Patrick Muana, 'The Revolutionary United Front of Sierra Leone: A Revolt of the Lumpenproletariat', in Clapham (ed.), *African Guerillas*.

[13] Martin Oppenheimer, *Urban Guerrilla* (London: Penguin, 1969), p. 42; see also Keen, *The Economic Functions of Violence in Civil Wars*, p. 48.

[14] Oppenheimer, *Urban Guerrilla*, p. 42.

[15] Abdullah and Muana, 'The Revolutionary United Front of Sierra Leone', p. 174.

[16] *Ibid.*

[17] Author's visit to NPFL headquarters, July 1994.

[18] *Ibid.*

[19] Interview with Gibril Foday-Mussa, Freetown, September 2001.

[20] Alao *et al.*, *Peacekeepers, Politicians and Warlords*, pp. 21 and 108; Ellis, 'Liberia's Warlord Insurgency', pp. 16–66.

21 John Hirsch, 'War in Sierra Leone', *Survival*, vol. 43, no. 3, Autumn 2001, pp. 146–51.

22 Interview with Dennis Bright, Commission for Conciliation and Peace, Freetown, September 2001.

23 This metaphor was used frequently among defence advisers in Freetown to describe the rise to power of the RUF; interviews, September 2001.

24 These statements concerned his visit to Nigeria, his spell in gaol and subsequent release and his second period as a prisoner. Interview with Dennis Bright.

25 Sierra Leone Editorial Committee, *Sierra Leone Heroes: Fifty Great Men and Women Who Helped To Build the Nation* (London: Commonwealth Printers, 1988), p. 42.

26 Interview with international advisory staff, Freetown, September 2001.

27 Interview with Defence Attaché, Freetown, September 2001.

28 Abdullah and Muana, 'The Revolutionary United Front of Sierra Leone', p. 188.

29 *Ibid.*

30 Interview with former SLA member 'Captain Blood', recently battle adjutant of the West Side Boys, Freetown, September 2001.

31 Interviews with former RUF warriors including 'Captain Blood', Freetown, September 2001. In June 2001, it was reported that a senior commander in the RUF was severely beaten, and then released to continue serving. Interview, Freetown, September 2001.

32 Interview with an officer of the SLA, who was for several years in the RUF. Olu A. Gordon, editor of *PEEP*, Freetown, maintains that drugs such as Ephadrine are also used to induce an adrenaline rush and that, in 1997, a consignment of this drug was stolen by the RUF for this purpose.

33 A spoof version on 29 May 2000, for example, described itself as a New Format for a New Lion News, and proceeded to ask awkward questions of the RUF leadership about poor living conditions in Makeni.

34 Some insist on the bonding value of wearing similar clothing; former warriors maintain that uniformity of clothing or colour helps to identify who is not in the unit, especially in the melee of an attack on a village.

35 In units which have been static for a while, and where boredom is becoming a problem, recreational brutality towards captured civilians may become a feature of the unit *pote*. Interview with Defence Attaché, Freetown, September 2001.

36 Duffield, 'Post-Modern Conflict', p. 17.

37 Alao *et al.*, *Peacekeepers, Politicians and Warlords*.

38 During the formal small-arms training that former RUF cadres receive when they opt to serve in the restructured SLA, it appears that individual fighters have a tendency to shut their eyes when they press the trigger. This may be caused by the habit of firing the weapon into the air while it is held across the body, as opposed to while it is against the shoulder. When the muzzle is closer to the face, the blast of gases is more intense and will, if repeated, tend to induce the firer to close their eyes automatically on pressing the trigger. Interview with International Military Advisory Training Team staff, Freetown, September 2001.

39 Sam Gbaydee Doe, 'Call Me By My Real Name: A Cry for Lost Identity', *Relief and Rehabilitation Network Newsletter*, no. 12, November 1998, p. 1.

40 During the occupation of the Cotlington University, Gbarnga, campus by the NPFL, Professor Delvin Walker observed the brutalisation and indoctrination of recruits. Alao *et al.*, *Peacekeepers, Politicians and Warlords*, Chapter 5.

41 The important exceptions are the urban Lumpens, particularly the *mooryan* in Mogadishu. Roland Marchal, 'Forms of Violence and Ways To Control It in an Urban War Zone: The Mooryan in Mogadishu', in H. Adam and R. Ford (eds), *Mending Rips in the Sky: Options for Somali Communities in the 21th Century* (Lawrenceville, NJ: Red Sea Press, 1997), pp. 193–209.

42 Seifulaziz Milas, 'Causes and Consequences of the Somalia Conflict', report prepared for the UNHCR, Nairobi, 11 February 1997, pp. 1, 2.

43 *Ibid.*

44 *Ibid.*

45 Even INGOs have in some cases become a dependency of a particular clan or family for every aspect of their accommodation, protection and staffing. *Ibid.*, p. 5.

46 Bernard Helander, 'The Somali Family', report from a conference held at Uppsala University, Sweden, March 1991, cited in Milas, 'Causes and Consequences of the Somalia Conflict', p. 3.

47 *Ibid.*, p. 3.

48 Interviews with Randolph Kent, Director of UNDP Somalia, Nairobi May 2001.

49 *Ibid.*

50 For example, see *Human Development Report 2001* (New York: UNDP, 2001), p. 58.

51 Marchal, 'Forms of Violence and Ways To Control It', p. 198.

52 *Ibid.*, pp. 200 and 201.

53 *Ibid.*

54 *Ibid.*, p. 196.

55 See John Masters, *Bugles and a Tiger* (London: Michael Joseph, 1956); H. Gibbs, *Historical Record of the Sixth Gurkha Rifles* (Aldershot: Gale and Polden, 1955), Chapter 2.

56 Marchal, 'Forms of Violence and Ways To Control It', p. 195.

57 Video footage of *mujahideen* ambushes of Soviet convoys in the 1980s supports accounts of extremely poor marksmanship and use of ground. Military historian Richard Holmes confirms that *mujahideen* leaders found it hard to control the exuberance of their fighters, who in the heat of contact would rise from their fire positions to hurl abuse at their enemy. Interview with Richard Holmes, Royal College of Military Science, Shrivenham, February 2002.

58 UK MoD, 'Counter-Revolutionary Operations', pp. 12 and 13.

59 In 1977, British doctrine reduced the motivating reasons for an uprising to: 'nationalism', 'racial or tribal rivalry', 'extremes of wealth and poverty' and 'maladministration and government corruption'. Twenty years later, these motives had been only slightly refined, to include 'religious' causes and 'neo-colonialism [referring to] the control of key sectors of the economy by foreign business interests, or the presence of allied troops and their bases under the terms of an unpopular treaty'.

60 Ernest den Haag, *Political Violence and Civil Disobedience* (New York: Harper Torchbooks, 1972), pp. 20 and 21.

61 Tamil resistance energy can be traced back to the 1956 'Sinhala Only' Bill passed by Sirimavo Bandaranaike's government. M. R. Narayan Swamy, *Tigers of Lanka*, second edition (Colombo: Vijitha Yapa Bookshop, 1996), Chapter 2.

62 *Ibid.*, p. 40.

63 Rohan Gunaratna, *War and Peace in Sri Lanka* (Colombo: Institute of Fundamental Studies, 1987), p. 6. See also Swamy, *Tigers of Lanka*, p. 59. Prabhakaran's constitution was developed in the late 1970s by five members of the central committee. It calls for a casteless Tamil state and the dissolution of the LTTE once this state is founded. All members were expected to sign.

64 See Frank Kitson, *Low-Intensity Operations* (London: Faber and Faber, 1971), p. 128.

65 Crystal Procyshen, 'Islam, Institutions and Insurgency: Territorial and Network Jihad', *Conflict, Security and Development*, vol. 1, no. 3, 2001, p. 42.

66 Information for most of this section is taken from interviews with senior officers in the Sri Lankan Police Special Task Force, May 2001.

67 Gunaratna, *War and Peace in Sri Lanka*, pp. 19 and 23.

68 *Ibid.*, p. 20.

69 Procyshen, 'Islam Institutions and Insurgency', p. 43.

70 Interview with Tamil nationalists, Colombo, May 2001.

71 Gunaratna, *War and Peace in Sri Lanka*, p. 19.

72 *Ibid.*, p. 42.

73 Procyshen, 'Islam, Institutions and Insurgency', p. 43.

74 Interview with Hannelie De Beer, South African National Defence Force, Johannesburg, 18 October 2001.

75 Swamy, *Tigers of Lanka*, p. 59.

76 Gunaratna, *War and Peace in Sri Lanka*, p. 20; and William Dalrymple, *The Age of Kali* (London: HarperCollins, 1999), p. 248.

77 Swamy, *Tigers of Lanka*, p. 60.

78 An indirect-fire weapon is registered by hitting the selected targets prior to an attack or defence to ensure accuracy before the actual operation commences. Silent registration involves making the calculations from a map without actually firing. Prabhakaran is known to carry out the calculation phase prior to an attack by sending out GPS operators dressed in civilian clothes. Interview with defence attachés, Colombo, May 2001.

79 *Ibid.*, p. 254; and interviews with Sri Lankan Police Special Task Force.

80 Dalrymple, *The Age of Kali*, p. 249.

81 *Ibid.* Many visitors and commentators have remarked on Prabhakaran's passion for Clint Eastwood films.

82 The precise reference for this manual is not available. It is called *Confronting the Enemy*, and is translated from Tamil for the Sri Lankan Armed Forces. See Gunaratna, *War and Peace in Sri Lanka*, pp. 50–51.

83 Procyshen, 'Islam, Institutions and Insurgency', pp. 43–50.

84 There is little evidence that the members of bin Laden's movement refer to themselves as 'the al-Qaeda', not least because of the banality of the image in comparison to more inspirational titles that speak of 'liberation', 'democracy', 'brotherhood' and even, as with *Sendero Luminoso* in Peru, a 'Shining Path'. However, in deference to prevailing usage al-Qaeda is used here to refer to bin Laden's network organisation.

85 These include all predominately Muslim countries such as Egypt, Pakistan, Afghanistan, Sudan, Somalia and Turkey, as well as secular states in which there is a Muslim first- or second-generation migrant community, such as the US, UK, France and Canada. According to the CIA, the total is now 63 countries. Ed Blanche, 'The Labyrinthian Money Trail of Osama bin Laden', *The Middle*

East, January 2002, p. 23; and Nick Fielding, 'The Network', *Sunday Times*, 18 November 2001, p. 4.

86 Robinson, *Bin Laden: Behind the Mask of the Terrorist*, p. 50.

87 *Ibid.*, p. 122.

88 For a review of bin Laden's utterances, see 'The World and Its Woes According to Osama bin Laden', *Sunday Times*, 22 September 2001, p. 22.

89 Bin Laden was a supporter of the London club Arsenal. See Robinson, *Bin Laden*, p. 168.

90 Bhupendra Jasani, 'Orbiting Spies: Opportunities and Challenges', *Space Policy*, 18 (2002), pp. 9–13.

91 Adam Robinson claims that al-Qaeda was ready for the reprisals, and that before the attack, during summer 2001, training programmes were speeded up, camps and supplies were shifted to remoter places and a structure of alternative HQ sites was prepared for a more dispersed operating profile. Robinson, *Bin Laden*, p. 283.

92 *Ibid.*, p. 92.

93 *Ibid.*, p. 97.

94 The destinations of the majority of the fighters were: Saudi Arabia (5,000); Yemen (3,000); Egypt (2,000); Algeria (2,800); Tunisia (400); Iraq (370); Libya (200); and a balance dispersed to Jordan, the United Arab Emirates, Sudan, Lebanon, Syria and Western countries. The estimated total is between 15,000 and 22,000. Robinson, *Bin Laden*, pp. 113–14.

95 Robinson maintains that, after the collapse of the Bank of Credit and Commerce International (BCCI), bin Laden became the banker for many popular Islamic insurgent movements. Robinson, *Bin Laden*, p. 138. In a similar vein, Ed Blanche describes al-Qaeda as the 'Ford Foundation of Terrorism', referring to its enabling role towards other movements that required its financial or technical support for a particular operation. Blanche, 'The Labyrinthian Money', pp. 22–24.

96 Oxford Analytica, 16 January 2002; and Robinson, *Bin Laden*, p. 203.

97 Oxford Analytica, 16 January 2002.

98 *Ibid.*

99 Robinson, *Bin Laden*, pp. 203–204.

100 These included many small private banks and high-street branches in Austria (Vienna), Malaysia, Hong Kong, the UK (London), Italy (Milan), the US (New York), Germany (Frankfurt) and Dubai. Peter Bergen, 'The Bin Laden Trial: What Did We Learn?', *Studies in Conflict and Terrorism*, no. 24, 2001, pp. 429–34. Blanche, 'The Labyrinthian Money Trail', p. 22.

101 Oxford Analytica, 16 January 2002.

102 'NATO Unmasks Fleet of Al Qaeda Merchantmen', *Sea Power*, February 2002.

103 Robinson, *Bin Laden*, p. 138.

104 Josh Meyer and Eric Lichtblau, 'Response To Terror', *Los Angeles Times*, 30 January 2002.

105 Blanche, 'The Labyrinthian Money Trail', p. 24.

106 Bruce Crumley, 'Terror's Little Helpers', *Time Atlantic*, vol. 159, issue 7, 18 February 2002, p. 28.

107 *Ibid.*

108 'Method to the Madness', *Newsweek*, vol. 138, issue 17, 22 October 2001, p. 54.

109 Nick Fielding, 'The Network', *Sunday Times*, 16 December 2001, p. 13.

110 See, for example, 'Britain's al Qaeda Connections', 29 January 2002, news.bbc.co.uk/hi/english/newsid

111 Nick Fielding, 'Encyclopaedia of Terror', *Sunday Times*, 4

November 2001, p. 5; and M. Franchetti, 'Severed Head Video', *ibid.*, 16 December 2001, p. 13. Despite the sensationalist tone of this report, it does confirm the extent of the use of video for training.

112 Edward Luttwak, *Coup d'Etat* (London: Penguin Books, 1969), Chapter 4.

113 *Ibid.*, Chapter 5.

Conclusion

1 Keegan, *A History of Warfare*, pp. 12–17.

2 Correctness, and the need to co-opt the reluctant support of many other functional areas and disciplines besides the military, will ensure a more anodyne nomenclature, but its effect will nevertheless be: to counter insurgency.